NEW YORK'S
5o BEST

Places
to Keep
Your Spirit
Alive

*A Guide to Renewing
the Body, Mind and Soul*

Beth Donnelly Cabán and Andrea Martin
with Allan Ishac

A CITY & COMPANY GUIDE • NEW YORK

Dedication

To the Divine Spark in Everyone.
Namasté.

Acknowledgments

Deep thanks to all whose ideas and support enabled us
to triumph through this project, especially Allan, Caitlin,
Erica, Helene, John, and Kimberly.

Library of Congress Cataloging-in Publication Data
is available upon request.
ISBN 1-929439-00-8
First Edition
Printed in the United States of America

Special editions of City & Company guides can be created to
specification. For details, contact the Special Sales Director at:
City & Company, 22 West 23rd Street, New York, NY 10010.

PUBLISHER'S NOTE:
Neither City & Company nor the authors have any interest,
financial or personal, in the locations in this book. No fees
were paid or services rendered in exchange for inclusion in
these pages. While every effort was made to ensure accuracy
at the time of publication, it is advisable to call ahead to
confirm current addresses and specific information.

10 9 8 7 6 5 4 3 2 1

Contents

6 Preface

8 Introduction

10 A Course in Miracles
Find a path back to God

12 All Souls Church
Explore life's questions in rich conversation

14 Asian Classics Institute
Discover Buddhism's bountiful wisdom

16 Body and Soul
Sweat out tension and ignite your passion

18 Bowery Mission
Raise another's hopes, elevate your own

20 Brooklyn Women's Martial Arts
Feeling safe frees the spirit

22 Cathedral of St. John the Divine
Celebrate the wonder of life in all its diversity

24 Center for Book Arts
Transform your life into a spiritual work of art

26 Change Your Mind Day
Loving kindness on the Great Hill

28 College of Mount St. Vincent
A saintly place for nature's soothing pace

30 Congo Square Drummers Circle
Rhythms of release pulsate under the trees

32 Congregation B'nai Jeshurun Synagogue
A rebirth of a sacred community

34 First Church of Religious Science
Develop your ear for God's intuitive messages

36 Greenthumb Community Gardens
Work with the soil, nourish your soul

38 Habitat for Humanity
A concrete way to refurbish your spirit

40 **Healing Works**
The benefits of holistic health offered free of charge

42 **Hindu Temple**
Create a sacred altar and alter your consciousness

44 **Institute for Integrative Nutrition**
Radical nourishment for the soul

46 **Integral Yoga Institute**
Stretch yourself toward a more radiant life

48 **International Tae Kwon-do Center**
Practice the way of the peaceful warrior

50 **Jivamukti Yoga Center**
The rapture of yoga

52 **Kabbalah Center**
Mystical Jewish wisdom unveiled

54 **Kelly's Temple**
Harlem's most rousing gospel gathering

56 **Labyrinth Walks**
Step onto the path of tranquility

58 **Laughter Meditation**
The city's silliest soulwork

60 **Marble Collegiate Church**
The birthplace of positive thinking

62 **Mentoring Partnership of New York**
Share your greatest gifts

64 **Metropolitan Community Church**
God's love delivered judgment-free

66 **Metropolitan Museum of Art**
A gathering of the Gods on Fifth Avenue

68 **Mount Manresa Jesuit Retreat Center**
Reclaim, restore, renew...RETREAT!

70 **Moving Center-Gabrielle Roth**
Dance and live deeper

72 **New York Haiku-kai**
A taste of heaven in seventeen syllables

74 **New York Insight Meditation**
Inhale, exhale, and calm will prevail

76 **New York Open Center**
Epicenter of spiritual learning

78 **92nd Street Y**
Where the mind never stops learning

80 **Noonday Concert Series**
Squeeze some harmony into your lunch hour

82 **Poets House**
Uplift the human spirit through poetry

84 **Religious Society of Friends**
Find yourself in a sea of silence

86 **Riverside Church**
Review your life from the top down

88 **Sanctuary Restaurant**
Food for the spiritually hungry

90 **Statue of Liberty and Ellis Island**
Symbols of the quest for freedom

92 **Sufi Books**
A mecca for spiritual pilgrims

94 **Sweet Honey in the Rock**
A cappella divas who rock your soul

96 **The Tarot School**
Become a psychic, read your future

98 **Terry Schreiber Studio**
Play the leading role in your own discovery

100 **Union Square Green Market**
Root yourself in Mother Earth's abundance

102 **United Nations Temple of Understanding**
A sweeping spiritual tour

104 **Village Zendo**
Meditate with a modern-day master

106 **World Music Institute**
Caretaker of the world's most sacred music

108 **The Spa Experience**
Stone Spa
Millefleurs Day Spa
El Noël Wellness Center Day Spa
Carapan
Soho Sanctuary

Preface

During the year that Andrea and Beth were working on this book, we often talked about what it means to keep the spirit alive, renewed, and refreshed. For me, it's about finding ways to feel closer to God. I love the sense of peace and purpose that connection to a Higher Power offers me.

But like so many New Yorkers, I get spiritually lost and depleted easily. I'm a seeker distracted from my search by a stressful commute and a decision-a-minute day job. I lose my center as I rush to meet friends for dinner, cram a half-hour workout into an increasingly shorter day, or answer a dozen late night e-mails.

Still, I never totally lose sight of what I'm looking for. I take my little faith and I keep searching. Every day I hope for those glorious micro-moments when my spirit feels larger than the details of my busy life. Those few seconds of clarity and expansiveness are a vital source of renewal and refreshment.

When I wrote *New York's 50 Best Places to Find Peace and Quiet* a few years ago, I was motivated largely out of my need to find serene urban sanctuaries. I was looking for places where the incessant noise of the city was muted, where I could actually get enough quiet to hear God's guidance and intuitive messages. This became the core of my spiritual practice, and it's still an effective way for me to reconnect to my higher self.

But I know there are many other methods for accessing the spiritual side, for experiencing rejuvenation and renewal. When Andrea and Beth—both sincere and dedicated seekers—asked me to edit their inspiring book, I thought it would be an opportunity to enrich and expand my own search. And it has been.

Walking any path today is different than it was in the time of Buddha, or Mohammed, or Jesus. The real question for me is not how to live my life like the great masters once did, but how to live like the masters would if they came to earth now—born in New York City at the dawn of the third millennium. I want to know how Jesus would renew his spirit packed on the No. 6 train at rush hour.

That's what this book is all about: a sampling of possibilities, practical approaches, and accessible places where you can start or continue a quest for spiritual aliveness right now. Whether you have an hour, a day, or the rest of your life to dedicate to this search, you will find just the right avenues here.

If you've been yearning for richer spiritual experiences, I invite you to explore this valuable book. It reflects Andrea and Beth's respect and passion for sacred journeys, as well as their understanding that there is a unique way for everyone. And in New York, that way is often just around the corner.

Allan Ishac

Introduction

Something is going on in this city. More and more
New Yorkers are turning their personal searches
inward, looking for inner peace, inspiration, authentic-
ity, and a deeper sense of God.

With a passion and vitality unique to New Yorkers,
we're engaging in yoga classes, meditation practices,
healing circles, and altar building like never before.
We have become a city of seekers searching for the
sacred, determined to combat the daily grind of New
York living by recharging our spirits. We want to experience moments of greater expansiveness, open heart-
edness, appreciation, and awe, and we're doing it by
keeping our spirits renewed, ignited, alive.

There is simply no better place to keep your spirit
alive than in New York. Because along with our
extraordinary multiculturalism comes a rich multi-spiri-
tualism. Somewhere in the five boroughs, every traditional and unorthodox devotional practice on earth
has found a home. New York City could be called the
spiritual capital of the world.

Writing this book gave us a chance to "empty our
cups" and become soul-seekers in the city for one
incredible year. As devoted yoga practitioners ourselves, we went out to find not just the heart but the spirit and soul of New York. What we discovered is that
there is no one path to enlightenment. And that New
Yorkers should rejoice because we have every path to
pick from.

Traditional churches, yoga ashrams, improvisational dance centers, Reiki healing circles, meditation practices, martial arts schools, laughter workshops, miracles seminars, retreat weekends, drummers' groups, and intuition development classes—all hold the power and the promise to inspire and recharge your spirit. And the best of them are in this book.

New York City is famous for its materialism, less so for its sanctity. But soul is powerfully present here—the city crackles with spiritual life. And while it is not our intention to compile a shopper's guide to spirituality, we do hope that this book will introduce you to some unexpected sources of comfort and connection, peace and passion, rejuvenation and renewal. In short, places to keep your spirit alive.

Just seek and you shall find.

Beth Donnelly Cabán and Andrea Martin

A Course in Miracles

Find a path back to God

In the late 1960's, Dr. Helen Schucman, a research psychologist at Columbia University Medical Center began hearing a voice. The voice said, "This is a course in miracles. Please take notes." Helen, an atheist whose training described people who heard voices as psychotic, was terrified. Secretly, she consulted a colleague in her department, Dr. Bill Thetford. He advised her to write down what the voice said.

And for the next seven years, she did. Helen acted as a scribe, recording the messages in secretarial shorthand, while Bill typed them. The voice identified itself as that of Jesus, come 2000 years later to "correct" the misunderstandings of his original teachings on Earth. The result is the three-volume *A Course in Miracles*.

The Course is not intended to be a new religion or the foundation of another church. It's an educational course designed to help you learn the power of forgiveness and remember God. Composed in elegant Shakespearean meter, it is a beautiful integration of psychology and spirituality. The three volumes (the main text, a workbook, and a teacher's manual) may not be readily comprehensible; guidance can help extract the Course's wisdom.

On Sunday mornings at Cami Hall, the Interfaith Fellowship convenes to clarify these teachings in an uplifting gathering that includes live music, guided meditation, a sharing of miracle stories, and a talk on the Course. While well-known author Marianne Williamson has popularized these concepts in her best-selling books and international lectures, the Interfaith Fellowship explores the material in much greater depth. The Sunday morning gatherings at Cami Hall, and a Course In Miracles study groups sponsored by Interfaith, are faithful to the original teachings and texts.

The origins of the Course are unbelievable to some, but when you read the books something tangible happens: many people report being brought to tears or feeling a presence that is "in them, but not of them." Suspend your disbelief, even your cynicism, and check out a Course in Miracles.

Interfaith Fellowship at Cami Hall
165 West 57th Street
bet. 6th & 7th Avenues
New York, NY 10019
Phone: 212-799-0986/914-496-9089

All Souls Church

Explore life's questions in rich conversation

What brings such a varied and independent group of people together at this Unitarian house of worship? The conversation and Minister Forrest Church. He likens this congregation to that of a little ancient village in the city. The intimate community counters the anonymity of our urban existence. This church has liberal Christian roots and transcendental wings. At All Souls your own experience is relevant and valued, and your questions are the fuel for life's richest journey—that of the spirit. You are not asked to accept someone else's revelation for your own. You are not asked to cede your freedom of mind. You come to be part of the conversation, to engage in illuminating ideas.

Forrest Church acknowledges with a smile, "There are no final answers to unanswerable questions. Have awe at how unbelievable it is to be alive. Have humility that we are all alike in what we don't understand. Use reason, our human tools, to process this world. Bring mutual respect to the conversation; there is one light shining through many windows."

The Lifelines Center, a spin-off project of All Souls Church, takes the conversation to another setting. As its name suggests, its goal is to create lifelines among people—linking hands, hearts, and minds. The Lifelines Center's mission is to restore communities, which nourish our sense of meaning and support our sense of purpose. The center fosters human connection and interaction around the primary issues that shape our lives. With no ideological or political bias, it offers programs relating to work, love, society, and spirit.

Both All Souls and the Lifelines Center use the Internet as a tool to widen their reach. The All Soul's website posts full-text versions of the past months' sermons, and the Lifelines Center's website is a hub where people can connect to others who are searching for meaning in their lives. In person or in cyberspace, All Souls Church and the Lifelines Center succeed in facilitating connection, fostering an environment of mutual respect, common ground, and reverence for life. Accept the invitation to join this community of inquisitive souls.

1157 Lexington Avenue at 80th Street
New York, NY 10021
Phone: 212-535-5530
www.allsoulsnyc.org
Lifelines Center
Phone: 212-988-1708
www.lifelinescenter.org

Asian Classics Institute

Discover Buddhism's bountiful wisdom

The Asian Classics Institute (ACI) is quite a remarkable resource. Among the wealth of programs and organizations that illuminate the many paths of the Buddhist tradition here in the city, ACI is perhaps the most comprehensive. It encourages and supports the serious study and personal practice of the original teachings of Buddha.

Michael Roach, the founder of the Asian Classics Institute, holds the title of Geshe, or Master—a title bestowed upon him after he completed the eighteen-year coursework to become a Master in Buddhist philosophy. Roach, the first westerner to become a Geshe, was so enriched by his learning, he felt it imperative that others have the same opportunity for study. He wanted to translate the teachings so fellow westerners could delve as deeply into the Buddha's wisdom as he had.

This desire has become the mission of the ACI where, over the years, Roach's students (who study the Tibetan language at the Institute) have translated and transcribed the original Buddhist scriptures from Tibetan into English. Today the texts and coursework are available in printed form, CD-ROM, and on the web.

To get a sense of the Asian Classics Institute's style and offerings, visit the General Studies class on Friday nights. There is no commitment required; you come when you can. The Institute also offers regular meditation and Tibetan language classes weekly at the affiliated Three Jewels Bookstore on East 5th Street.

What sets the Asian Classics Institute apart from other study centers is its seven-year formal education program—a teacher training and translation program—that involves study of the original Buddhist scriptures, rigorous meditation practice, and retreats. If you ever wanted to get deeply rooted in the Buddha's teaching without becoming a monk or nun or getting a Ph.D., this may be the best opportunity. The course is structured so that you can hold a job, and have a family and a social life, while maintaining serious commitment to your studies.

You might wonder how much this all costs considering the time and money invested in obtaining, translating, transcribing, duplicating, and distributing the sacred teachings. In Buddhism, the dharma—the teachings of the Buddha—are considered priceless and thus offered for free. In fact, in the monasteries of Tibet, India, and Mongolia, the teacher is responsible for covering their students' expenses. ACI honors that ancient system: all ACI teachings, courses, even the formal study program—including the reading materials—are free of charge. Donations from corporations, foundations, students, generous souls, and good karma help make ends meet.

P.O. Box 20373
New York, NY 10009
Phone: 212-475-7752
www.world-view.org

Body and Soul

Sweat out tension and ignite your passion

What's a dance club doing in a book about keeping your spirit alive? The name Body and Soul should give you a clue as to its potential to do just that—so read on.

Body and Soul is the afternoon dance party at the club Vinyl every Sunday, from 3 p.m. until midnight. In the way a prophet has disciples, this place has ritual followers who come every weekend to sweat out their tension and awaken their passion. They come here to dance fiercely. It is a temple of movement, and music is the divine voice.

This legendary party attracts an eclectic mix of faithfuls, dancing to signature house music, Latin sounds, and garage rock classics. People come to take a pilgrimage inward, to find the kinetic crowd connection that only a dance floor can inspire.

Body and Soul is about abandonment, shedding inhibitions, and being in your own groove. The space is huge, dimly lit, and hot from expended energy; check your ego and your vanity at the door, and wear the bare minimum because here it's about dancing and the magnificent river of sweat it creates—not primping and pretense.

Historically, every culture has used dance to transform the soul. The Body and Soul experience is our version of pure sensation, connection, and rhythm. Let your body's inherent musicality reveal itself.

Trust the DJ to carry you. In the middle of an intense Latin beat, the sound of the bass line pumps like thunder. The lights are flashing and suddenly the music stops, and it's still pounding. Everyone is drenched in this ecstatic moment, their arms outstretched to the sky. Every heart is broken open in the perfection of this movement. And the music starts again.

At Body and Soul, you lose all perception of time and space. You arrive in daylight and leave in darkness. Outside feels strange, like a new day. You have been lost, carried away, and reborn. You're hungry, ravenous, passionate, ready for the night ahead. And you're free.

6 Hubert Street at Hudson Street
New York, NY 10013
Phone: 212-343-1379
Sundays at Vinyl
Hours: 3pm-12 midnight

Bowery Mission

Raise another's hopes, elevate your own

For decades, The Bowery was considered America's boulevard of debauchery and despair, a notoriously dismal place that revealed the rotting underbelly of the human spirit. There was always plenty of misery on the Bowery, and no shortage of people with hands outstretched asking for money or something to eat.

Against this backdrop of grimness and poverty, the Bowery Mission began its service as our nation's oldest soup kitchen and homeless shelter. Staff and volunteers at the Bowery Mission have been serving hot meals, providing clean beds and warm showers, and offering compassion, hope, and guidance to New York's neediest souls for more than 120 years.

Many spiritual traditions teach that serving others is the path of a genuine seeker. When we serve the basic needs of another person we understand that if one of us suffers, we all suffer. The Bowery Mission is an extraordinary place to volunteer because the rewards of your service are immediate and personal. You'll have the satisfaction of seeing the simplest gestures have the greatest impact—the way a hot meal lifts a person's mood for the day or how a warm bed gives comfort for the night.

Over the past century, the Mission has grown into a comprehensive outreach program for men and women caught up in cycles of poverty, abuse, and addiction. These recovery programs succeed. In fact, most of the Mission's full-time staff are people who rose from despair on the streets to lives of self-respect, self-discipline, and self-reliance.

Most of the day-to-day activities at the Mission are performed by volunteers—ordinary people who share their time, compassion, and respect with those people most in need. As a volunteer, you can help prepare or serve meals—more than 250 men are fed each day at the men's center—or you can organize and distribute clothing to people who have been living on the streets.

Of course, there are thousands of valuable ways to be of service in this city, and choosing one that speaks to your heart is the key to making a difference. But the caring work done at the Bowery Mission is so practical and positive, and restores so much dignity, it's guaranteed to change at least one life forever: your own.

227 Bowery
New York, NY 10002
Phone: 212-674-3456
www.bowery.org

Brooklyn Women's Martial Arts

Feeling safe frees the spirit

Have you ever walked down a street alone, afraid because someone was walking too closely behind you? Did you cross the street wishing for the strength to overcome your vulnerability? Or maybe you pulled your belongings closer to you and wondered if danger was really approaching.

Founded in 1974, Brooklyn Women's Martial Arts set out to change that fear. A vehicle for women's empowerment and a place to heal from violence, the idea for the center grew out of the political energy of the 60s. At this school, women and children study self-defense in order to build their physical strength as well as their self-confidence.

The Okinawan style of karate taught here is called Goju. This form uses breath and movement as ways to develop focus. Hard kicks and punches combine with soft, fluid motions that originate from the energy in your center. Goju is a spiritual practice originally used by monks in China to develop physical and mental strength. The practice involves katas (a choreographed series of movements), sparring (controlled physical matches with a partner), and meditation.

A palpable energy force builds during each class. This "energy pool," borne from the efforts of all the individuals present, has the power to renew you physically, mentally, emotionally, and spiritually. A commitment to eradicating the conditions which breed violence creates a fierce bond between participants in classes. And that connection is empowering.

No one—woman, man, or child—should have to live in fear. If your spirit has been broken by the threat or reality of violence, Brooklyn Women's Martial Arts, as well as many other martial arts academies throughout the city, can give you new tools for self-empowerment. An absence of fear naturally expands our spirits, frees our minds, and opens our hearts, allowing us to move forward with our dreams.

The Center for Anti-Violence Education
421 Fifth Avenue at 9th Street
Brooklyn, NY 11215
Phone: 718-788-1775

Cathedral of
St. John the Divine

Celebrate the wonder of life in all its diversity

Vibrant banners hang at the doors of St. John the Divine proclaiming, "This is a place to begin, a time to renew. All are welcome here."

The Cathedral of St. John the Divine's magnificence rests not only in its spectacular architecture (it is the largest Gothic structure in the world), but also in the spirit that reverberates here. The vastness of the Cathedral—its vaulted ceiling reaches high into the heavens—seems to provide an immediate link to the Divine. From its fortress-like perch atop Cathedral Heights, you can greet the rising sun over Morningside Park, bask in its midday rays, or bid it farewell as it sets in the West.

St. John the Divine has been called "the Living Cathedral," and life in all its diverse wonder is honored here. This building is one of the most ecumenical religious institutions on earth—a house of prayer for all creatures great and small. Musician Paul Winter called it "a place of pilgrimage, a very affirming, encouraging place regardless of your spiritual persuasions."

Whether it's the sight of a camel lumbering down the aisle for the blessing of the animals on the Feast Day of St. Francis, or the sound of the great pipe organ or of a noted speaker or performer that brings you into the church, every ritual is meant to exhilarate and rejuvenate you. Here religion is brought down to earth while still letting your spirit soar.

Two of the Cathedral's most spectacular celebrations are Paul Winter's Summer and Winter Solstice Concerts. Since 1980, these concerts have become a traditional marking of the earth's cyclical dance. The solstices are the most universal milestones in the year. People from all spiritual traditions can celebrate the miracle and diversity of life on earth during the solstice.

Paul Winter's group, the Consort weaves together rich musical rhythms and textures from around the world. Gongs, bells, and drums blend with the complex voices of nature—such as humpback whales and wolves—all spilling into a kind of jazz. The result, as the sounds resonate in the cavernous space of the Cathedral, is a supernatural reverie that can reawaken any of your hibernating senses. These magical nights of darkness and light transform listening into a spiritual experience.

Wander through the Cathedral, its spaces speckled with heavenly stained glass light. See the musings of a forlorn prisoner tacked to the Poetry Wall; or the rusty old saxophone through which John Coltrane used to blow his meditations; or a crocus emerging from the earth in the Biblical Garden; or the regal peacock parading his feathered train around the grounds. It's all a reminder that everyone has their own special place in this "Living Cathedral."

1047 Amsterdam Avenue at 112th Street
New York, NY 10025
Phone: 212-662-2133
www.stjohndivine.org

Center for Book Arts

Transform your life into a spiritual work of art

In her groundbreaking book *The Artist's Way*, Julia Cameron links creativity to spirituality and argues that creative expression is the natural direction of life. Her book will do nothing less than convince you that "as we are creative beings, our lives become our works of art."

If creativity is, in fact, a path to self-realization, then we're all in luck. Throughout this city, densely populated with artists, are wonderful art schools offering instruction, inspiration, and reassuring creative camaraderie.

The Center for Book Arts is one haven where you can unfurl your creative sails. At this loft-space studio you'll find lifelong artists and novices at work in the traditional book arts: bookbinding, papermaking, letterpress printing, collage, lithography, and calligraphy. In small classes, you'll work closely with professional artists who make a life and a living from these crafts. Study the time-honored technique of Japanese bookbinding, create a photo journal, or even a high-tech electronic book complete with light and sound effects.

In the Center's fully-equipped hand bindery and letterpress print shop, the bookbinding processes are unveiled. You'll learn how paper and board and thread and glue all come elegantly together. Hand binding involves patience since the transformation is slow; when you work, the repetition of folding, cutting, marking, and sewing, all calm the mind. As you make decisions about shape, size, color, design, and text, you access the creativity that lives in you. The satisfaction of holding a book you've made with your own hands is the unique joy of being an artist.

The Center for Book Arts is just one place to nurture your creativity. The Coalition of New York City Community Schools of the Arts is an on-line listing of the city's best art schools. (www.nycommunityarts.org) Give shape to a lump of clay, make a sax sing, or cover a canvas with all your colors. At this web site you'll find all the resources you need to turn your life into a work of art.

When all your senses are fully engaged in creative work, your most inventive self comes out and plays and your truest dreams unfold. Plug yourself into the city's high-voltage current of creativity and ignite your soul.

28 West 27th Street, 3rd Floor
New York, NY 10001
Phone: 212-481-9853
www.centerforbookarts.org

Change
Your Mind Day

Loving kindness on the Great Hill

Can your spirit really be renewed in just one day? Yes—if you can find the right mix of inspiration, contemplation, meditation, and celebration. And we found it on an early summer day right at the top of Central Park. Change Your Mind Day, an annual event, brings it all together.

Change Your Mind Day, sponsored annually by *Tricycle Magazine: The Buddhist Review,* is in several cities nationwide each June. During the New York event, you'll hear composer Philip Glass, who performs here each year, filling the air with his ethereal melodies. If the sky could sing, it would rain these very sounds upon us.

With nearly a thousand people lying on the grass that carpets Central Park's Great Hill, the warm June sunshine, and an air of eagerness and mindfulness permeating the crowd, Change Your Mind Day offers a vast selection of teachers who will encourage you to contemplate the essence of your life. One of the highlights, a guided group meditation centering on the practice of "lovingkindness," quietly draws in sunbathers and soul-seekers alike. During this meditation practice, you send blessings and well wishes to an ever-widening circle of people. Starting with those closest to you—family and friends—you then expand outward to include strangers, acquaintances, even enemies. Eventually, the meditation broadens to encompass all beings on the planet.

Change Your Mind Day is a thought-provoking and peaceful way to spend a Saturday in the company of some of the world's most prominent Buddhist teachers. Though the roster changes each year, the power of the day has remained the same. Yes, it can be mentally challenging to embrace both friend and foe. Yet seldom do you experience a crowd sharing a singular thought, bound by a common purpose. And this experience just might be the one that soothes your weary mind.

c/o Tricycle Magazine
92 Vandam Street
bet. Hudson & Greenwich Streets
New York, NY 10013
Phone: 212-645-1143
www.tricycle.com

College of Mount St. Vincent

A saintly place for nature's soothing pace

When you leave the crush of the city, outdoor sanctuaries can become vital places to recover from a suffocated soul. A pristine mountaintop can become your meditation center, a towering forest your cathedral, and a silent lakeside clearing your personal temple.

It is an expansive feeling to contemplate Heaven under the heavens, or to praise God for the gifts of nature while in nature. But if you don't have the luxury of leaving the city as often as you'd like, the campus of the College of Mount St. Vincent—open to the public—is a rare and rewarding find.

This spectacular campus overlooking the Hudson River is a tribute to the lifework of Manhattan-born Elizabeth Seton—America's first saint. Seton lived at the time of our nation's revolution, and was a steadfast defender of the rights of the downtrodden. Among her miraculous acts was the creation of the parochial school system in America. The College of Mount St. Vincent was founded years later by Seton's religious order, the Sisters of Charity.

When the crush of downtown has you on overload, and Central Park is just too ... well, central, a quick trip to this sprawling, meticulously manicured college campus with its sweeping vistas of the Palisades across the river, is a convenient retreat. The grounds, with their storybook cobblestoned walkways and quaint bridges are designed for reflection and reverie. Elizabeth Seton delighted in nature's grandeur, and here you can lay back in lush, cool grass, marvel at a canopy of broad blue sky, or savor a meditative moment in one of the scattered grottos.

The shrine-like stone enclosures situated along walkways filled with flowers and illuminated with candles, are what make Mount St. Vincent seem so sacred. The grottos offer refuge and protection—safe quiet places to breathe slowly and think clearly. You sense the respectful presence of worshippers who have passed before you, lit their candles, said their prayers, and whispered their dreams. With these simple gestures they seem to have consecrated the grounds, creating a comforting place of healing and renewal.

The College of Mount St. Vincent is a divine, day-long excursion that can work wonders on your mood and spirit. Treat yourself to nature's tranquility for an afternoon, and you're bound to feel a little more saintly.

6301 Riverdale Avenue
Riverdale, NY 10471
Phone: 1-800-665-CMSV
www.cmsv.edu

Congo Square Drummers Circle

Rhythms of release pulsate under the trees

The sound of the drum is sacred; it is said to be imbued with spirit. Babatunde Olatunji, credited with introducing the rhythms and passion of African drumming to the West, says, "The spirit of the drum is something you feel when people come together to play. It's a feeling that makes you say to yourself, 'I'm glad to be alive today. I'm glad I'm here. I'm glad I'm part of this world.'" Need a dose of that kind of gratitude?

Every Sunday in Prospect Park from May to October, the Congo Square Drummers Circle rouses these life-affirming feelings. Bring along a drum or just drop by to check out the scene. Talented percussionists get together in the park from mid-morning until the sun begins to wane and neither heat nor rain will drive them away. If they're not at Drummer's Grove, just listen for the rhythm further down the road under the Concert Grove gazebo. During a summer shower, you can stand protected under its roof or dance in the rain.

Congo Square's Drummers Circle builds a pulsating house of worship, a congregation under the shade of trees. Sound like your kind of temple? Congas, bongos, djumbaks, djembes, flutes, shakers, rainmakers, and beating hands produce the Circle's incantations, while in the distance, a sultry Sunday saxophone brightens the park.

30

No sound has a more powerful effect on your consciousness (or subconscious) than the rhythmic pulse of a heartbeat. It is the surest sign of life. Blood pumping through the veins is the very first sound you heard in your mother's womb, and drumming is the ancient mimicking of these primordial rhythms of life. The drum's echo has the power and passion to reconnect you with an infinite collective consciousness.

If you've ever considered what your soul might sound like, the drum's beat may give you a clue. At the Congo Square Drummers Circle, listening happens with your whole body. Rhythm is a pulse that pounds in your heart and through your veins. This is the spirit of the drum.

Drummer's Grove
Prospect Park
Parkside/Ocean Avenue Entrance
Sundays mid May —October

Congregation B'nai Jeshurun Synagogue

A rebirth of a sacred community

In a letter written to its members in 1993, the rabbis at B'nai Jeshurun announced a goal for the year 2000. Their objective: the creation of *k'hillah k'doshah*, a sacred community. Have they lived up to their word? One visit to a Shabbat service on Friday night would resoundingly answer this question—absolutely.

Since the mid-1980s, this synagogue has been through a renaissance. At that time, there were not enough congregants for a Shabbat service. In 1985, the arrival of Rabbi Marshall T. Meyer, a magnetic rabbi who settled in New York City, began to energize the worshippers into the thriving congregation it is today. Meyer had already been instrumental in building a flourishing Jewish community in Argentina. Worshipping under the weight of fascist oppression there, he and his followers gained a full appreciation of the freedom to openly practice faith in God. Meyer carried that appreciation with him back to B'nai Jeshurun, where they don't take worship for granted.

If you're a non-practicing Jew, B'nai Jeshurun's exuberant expression of Judaism will make you wonder why you haven't been exploring your own heritage. Chanting in Sanskrit will suddenly seem odd, when you realize you could have been singing in Hebrew. Who knew?

Rabbis Bronstein and Matalon (who succeeded Marshall Meyer after his death) and Cantor Ari Priven, all hail from Meyer's original congregation. Individually inspiring and devoted, the rabbis form a charismatic team.

The Friday night Shabbat service is the bedrock of B'nai worship. It welcomes Saturday—the day of rest—with beautiful songs and prayer. You begin by celebrating the night as you would a bride, joining hands in a wedding dance, parading and singing through the isles to greet her. At this service you'll be swept into the fullness of this robust community just as you'll be swept into the line of worshipping dancers. The ritual of Friday night is to sing to God. Every word is a blessing that gives thanks and praises God, acknowledging his presence among us.

Once you've experienced B'nai's rebirth for yourself, you'll have become a part of the synagogue's newest challenge—how do you create an intimate place with so many people? Don't worry, they're already figuring it out.

257 West 88th Street
bet. West End Avenue & Broadway
New York, NY 10024
Phone: 212-787-7600
www.bj.org

First Church of Religious Science

Develop your ear for God's intuitive messages

There is a wonderful saying that prayer is the way we speak to God, and intuition is the way God speaks back.

According to the First Church of Religious Science, or the Science of Mind, intuition is the voice of God. If you listen closely, your intuition can become a reliable source for guidance; it can tell you when you need to make a change and how to make it. This is a manifestation of the power of a mind in touch with spirit.

According to the Science of Mind, the world and the Universal Spirit directing it work quite simply: you get what you ask for—nothing more, nothing less. If you absorb the negativity of the world around you without awareness, this same negativity tends to show up in your life. If you tune in to the positive energy of the world and cultivate positive thinking, your outer life reflects this, too. It sounds so easy, but how do you actually make such mind-altering changes?

The answer for Religious Scientists is a prayer-based method of meditation called "Spiritual Mind Treatments." According to Christian tradition, this is the kind of prayer that Christ used in his healings. In Spiritual Mind Treatments, you formulate your ideas for change into very specific, spoken requests or prayers.

The prayer reaffirms that we live in an abundant universe, and offers a way to cultivate positive thoughts and express your deepest longings. Committed, regular practicing of Spiritual Mind Treatments can recalibrate negative habits and thinking, letting intuition be a more guiding presence.

Philosophical yet practical, the Science of Mind (which is not to be confused with L. Ron Hubbard's Scientology or Christian Science) combines laws of science, philosophical theories, and religious revelations to heal, regenerate, and revolutionize your patterns of thinking. The Science of Mind approach is unique; you do not surrender to an already decided truth, instead you engage in thoughtful examinations of Christian texts to uncover their symbolic meanings. If you have a tendency to observe and analyze the world around you, this approach just might suit you.

You can join the community of Science of Mind seekers at Alice Tully Hall for Sunday worship. Regular Science of Mind classes also offer a concrete understanding of how to use your mind to cultivate the positive in your life and develop a keen ear for intuitive messages.

14 East 48th Street
bet. Madison & 5th Avenues
New York, NY 10017
Phone: 212-688-0600
e-mail: fcrsny@aol.com

Greenthumb Community Gardens

Work with the soil, nourish your soul

Most New Yorkers don't get enough earth. We get plenty of dirt, but it's not the right kind— the earthy loam under our fingernails from a day of digging or the mud on our pants from weeding between a row of lettuce heads.

Thanks to an organization called the Greenthumb Community Gardens, getting good earth isn't just reserved for country dwellers. Fervent urban gardeners who consider touching, turning, and tilling the earth as essential as eating and breathing are out there. Through Greenthumb, these folks have rediscovered a timeless secret: working with the soil nourishes the soul.

The simple miracles of nature are easy to see when you tend a garden. The fact that a seed—a little sleeping dot of life—can become a blooming bougainvillea, a bulbous ripe tomato, a pungent batch of basil, or a climbing morning glory is astonishing. Planting a city garden cultivates reverence for life. Finding ways to touch the soil, to see this wonder unfold regularly in New York's paved-over paradise, can deliver you to a unique place of delight and contentment.

Maybe you've happened upon a city garden—a pleasant surprise for your overtaxed senses. The smell of fertile earth, even for just one breath, is a welcome change from car exhaust. The sight of a corner transformed from a trash-strewn dump to a verdant green Eden or of rows of happy plants instead of parked cars in an empty alley makes you root for Mother Nature. In a saner city, every spot of unused ground would be resplendent with these chlorophylled bits of cared-for life.

The Greenthumb Community Gardens organization is successfully helping urban gardeners turn vacant lots into vibrant plots while building community in the process. Hundreds of New Yorkers have watered the earth with their sweat and joyful labor, producing lush urban oases in every borough. These gardens inspire conversation and friendship, and make our city a more nourishing place to live, walk, work, and breathe.

In your garden space, whether it's a window box, a sprawling rooftop terrace, or a resurrected Greenthumb parcel, creativity will flourish, and tranquility will reign. Here you and the earth can bond in a union that yields whatever you sow—ripe tomatoes, fragrant lilacs, even giant sunflowers. Call or contact the Greenthumb folks about joining a community garden in your neighborhood. In a city starving for it, gardening is right up there next to godliness.

49 Chambers Street at Broadway
New York, NY 10007
Phone: 212-788-8059

Habitat for Humanity

A concrete way to refurbish your spirit

Hammers, nails, electric drills, and circular saws—are these tools for renewing the spirit?

They are when you see the extraordinary work being done at Habitat for Humanity. Here practical creation, the manifestation of vision, the sweat and ache of physical labor, and the realization of a great American dream—the building of a home—can raise your spirit to new heights of purpose and fulfillment.

Why is this significant for those of us interested in nurturing our inner selves? Because a renewed spirit comes not only from talking about God, meditating, or studying scriptures. It arises most naturally from moments of meaningful connection, and, as many teachings tell us, it also arises from helping others.

Working with Habitat for Humanity—a nonprofit Christian ministry that deals with the issues of poverty, housing, and homelessness—is an opportunity to build and renovate homes for families in need and connect with fellow volunteers and future homeowners. Habitat's vision is to make "decent shelter a matter of conscience and action." The fruits of your labors are immediate and concrete; the service you provide is essential. Putting a sturdy roof over a family's head, quite possibly the first home they've ever owned, makes a profound impact on every life involved.

You don't need any particular skills to join the Habitat workforce, but if you have practical knowledge of construction, even better. In fact, as part of a Habitat team, you will learn valuable skills as well as reap personal rewards. One volunteer said, "I left with more at the end of the day than I had arrived with in the morning. I felt that I was part of something so much bigger than myself." Feeling connected to a larger truth is paramount in the life of every human being. Perhaps it is the essence of spiritual renewal.

You can join a Habitat project for an afternoon, a week, or a month. Work on a local project rebuilding row houses in Queens or join a Habitat International chapter anywhere from Armenia to Zimbabwe.

Working with Habitat for Humanity is a life-enhancing experience where more than just structures are built. Hammering a shingle on the roof of a two-room house can be one path to lifting the roof of your own soul.

334 Furman Street
Brooklyn, NY 11201
Phone: 718-246-5656
www.habitat—nyc.org

Healing Works

The benefits of holistic health offered free of charge

We have learned in recent years about the laying-on-of-hands and its ability to heal. Spiritually-guided loving touch has been shown to facilitate healing in post-operative patients. Premature babies make rapid progress when frequently touched, and "loving touch circles" are now an accepted form of cancer therapy. Clearly, the curative powers of touch can no longer be ignored.

Reiki—a Japanese word meaning unconditional love—is an ancient form of the laying-on-of-hands that can restore balance between your energy and the energy of the world around you. The principles of Reiki are reflected in the philosophy of Healing Works, a wellness center dedicated to providing health education and access to holistic health practitioners free of charge. Along with Reiki practitioners, the staff at Healing Works includes social workers, psychologists, couples therapists, nutritionists, yoga, meditation, and tai chi instructors, chiropractors, bereavement counselors, massage therapists, and acupuncturists.

Since 1994, Healing Works has amassed a network of more than 80 practitioners who volunteer their time for one-on-one sessions, classes, and workshops. All of the professionals who work in this center bring a holistic understanding of health to their practice. As they support you in healing mind, body, and spirit, they also support your capacity for growth and renewal. If you are searching for ways to restore balance in your life, in your relationships, or in your body, Healing Works provides a safe place to begin such explorations.

At the Thursday night Reiki Healing Circle, you can join a diverse mix of New Yorkers who fill the oversized couches, cushions, and chairs circling a cozy room. Some will be there for the first time to learn about Reiki, while others will have returned for another dose of the loving touch. The laying-on-of-hands might be just the thing to sooth your exhausted body, quiet your agitated mind, and mend your tired spirit.

Participating in the Reiki Healing Circle gives you a new understanding of the nature of love as energy and how we can actually send and receive unconditional love in our daily lives. Standing on the bus, packed together in the subway, even rushing past each other on the streets, it is possible to become a source of mutual support and renewal.

244 Fifth Avenue, 6th floor,
bet. 27th & 28th Streets
New York, NY 10001
Phone: 212-696-9144
www.healingworks.org

Hindu Temple

Create a sacred altar and alter your consciousness

Creating an altar—a sacred place to house your own personal devotional reminders—is an easy way to invoke the sacred. It signals the gods that you're ready to talk and willing to listen.

This is your temple to build, and what you use to build it will hold the key to opening your spiritual passageways every time you kneel or sit before it. These meaningful objects might consist of perfect stones you found on the beach, a bright yellow tulip cut from your window box, a sweet stick of incense, an encouraging note from a friend, a small statue, a precious piece of art, or a string of beads.

The Hindu Temple in Queens can inspire you to create your personal altar. The Temple's own altar is home to Ganesh. With the head of an elephant and the body of a human, Ganesh represents, in Hindu faith, the universality of creation. Here it is believed that all creation begins with sound, and that Ganesh is the primal sound "OM," out of which the universe was born. Ganesh is the remover of obstacles; with his long trunk he moves barriers from your path. Worshipping Ganesh is a way to seek divine support for succeeding in your endeavors.

A large statue of Ganesh sits in the alcove at the front of the Temple's prayer room. In the Sunday morning ritual devotion to the deity, the statue is bathed over and over again with steaming water, while Sanskrit chants are sung. Attending this service is like taking a mini-trip to India. The robed man pouring tin cupfuls of water down the stone body of the statue seems like a mystical apparition. This entire ritual is about repetition and devotion's rewards.

Devotion, known as Bhakti in the Hindu faith, is the primary path focused on at the Hindu Temple and in front of your altar. According to the Hindu Temple, intense devotion is the easiest path to God, the fast track. As explained at the Temple, worshipping the deity of your choice will help you relate to God. Supposedly, the consecrated idols, when worshipped consistently, acquire a capacity to respond. In other words, they show up to help.

You don't necessarily need to use Hindu deities for your altar. Adorn it with whatever calls forth your faith, and sanctify the experience with your own rituals. See what five minutes of devotion in front of your altar each day can do to alter your life.

Society of North America
45-57 Bowne Street
Flushing, NY 11355
Phone: 718-460-8484
1-(800) 99-HINDU
www.indianet.com/ganesh/

Institute for
Integrative Nutrition

Radical nourishment for the soul

The most radical idea at the Institute for Integrative Nutrition (IIN) is the way they define "diet." Here, they teach that diet consists of all the things that nourish and sustain us. Primarily, we are sustained by love. Not food, love. Emotional warmth, fulfilling work, caring touch, carefree play, joyful self-expression, and relaxation are primary sources of nourishment for the soul. Food is considered a secondary source of sustenance. The more primary nourishment we receive, the less dependent we are on food.

If you doubt this, consider your own life. When you feel lonesome, uninspired, dissatisfied, or depressed, do you turn to cookies to satiate emotional needs and spiritual cravings, only to cause more emptiness and imbalance? It was not always this way. Remember a time when you were falling passionately in love, or were deeply engaged in a meaningful project? Remember as a child, being full of curiosity, spontaneity, and energy? During those times, someone probably had to remind you to eat. Happiness, excitement, and zest for life sustained you.

In short, the IIN understanding of diet goes well beyond the foods you eat, or try not to eat. It represents an invitation to freedom from calorie counting, trend diets, limitations, and control. It helps you make changes in your diet and lifestyle that promote true health and balance. The programs and perspectives are radical, life affirming, and life changing. They take diet as a fundamental starting point for realigning and re-examining your entire life, your dreams, and your passions.

IIN's approach to keeping your spirit alive entirely negates media messages that promise the more you consume the better you'll feel. At IIN, holistic health counselors help you assess your diet and determine deficiencies or excesses in both your primary and secondary sources of nourishment. A balanced diet from this perspective takes into account the whole person—body, mind, spirit, lifestyle, and community. Then you're given the support you need as you begin to make changes in your life, and as you learn to care for, nurture, and nourish yourself and others.

At IIN you'll find a community of travelers on the lifetime journey toward true health, happiness, and freedom. One student recently said, "The way I have learned to take care of myself makes me feel like I am at a retreat or a spa. I love my life." And a love of life is the spirit emerging.

120 West 41st Street at 6th Avenue
New York, NY 10036
Phone: 212-730-5433
www.gullivers.org

Integral Yoga Institute

Stretch yourself toward a more radiant life

When was the last time you surrendered—not to an enemy but to yourself? Maybe you never have. Swami Satchidananda, founder of the Integral Yoga Institute (IYI), describes the rewards of self-surrender as "an easeful body, a peaceful mind, and a useful life."

Interested? Then join the wave of New Yorkers turning to yoga as a means for simultaneously reviving body, mind, and spirit. Today, nearly every neighborhood throughout the five boroughs has a yoga center. Yoga literally means "yoke," or union. Through yoga postures or asanas, practitioners are taught to reunite with the "body beyond the body." You achieve this goal by learning to breathe more fully and by developing a steady, focused mind. Deep, open breathing and a quiet mind can help you connect to your spiritual consciousness—a dynamic union with benefits that stretches beyond your knowing.

The seeds of these teachings were planted in Western soil more than 30 years ago when Spiritual Master Swami Satchidananda migrated to New York from India to establish the Integral Yoga Institute. These seeds have taken root and blossomed with a decidedly American flavor. Integral Yoga is practical, accessible, and comfortable.

Hatha yoga, one type of yoga practiced at IYI that works with the physical body, has been called yoga's passport to the West. Postures, breathing practices, deep relaxation, and chanting create a supple, relaxed body, increasing vitality and radiant health. Integral offers over 100 hatha yoga classes each week.

The word hatha can be translated as Sun (ha) and Moon (tha), or effort and surrender. While most of us have the "effort" part of the equation down, the Integral Yoga Institute has not forgotten the importance of surrender—the place where your practice actually begins. This is where you gain much by letting go. Yoga is about accepting who you are now, not who you'll be the day you can bury your face against your knees in a forward bend.

After elbowing your way through the city, laying your worn out body on IYI's softly carpeted Gold Room floor might be the first step toward perfect union between your tired, moody, ordinary self, and your highest, most extraordinary divine Self.

Downtown Center: 227 West 13th Street
bet. 7th & 8th Avenues
New York, NY 10011
Phone: 212-929-0586
Uptown Center:
200 West 72nd Street at Broadway
New York, NY 10023
Phone: 212-721-4000
www.IntegralYogaofNewYork.org

International Tae Kwon-Do Center

Practice the way of the peaceful warrior

Have you ever encountered someone with such amazing physical prowess and discipline that you were motivated to get in shape now? The *Rocky* movies of the 1970s and 1980s sent thousands of us out for new running shoes, and we triumphantly scaled steps in search of newfound reserves of strength, stamina, and self-confidence.

Peering through the glass doors of the International Tae Kwon-Do Center on 13th Street inspires this kind of awe and determination. Your body responds to what your eyes see—the strength and grace of students in action.

Tae Kwon-Do is the Korean form of self-defense. Originating in the 1300s, the name translates as the art of kicking and punching. But don't be misled; the magic of the practice lies in its unswerving commitment to non-violence. The entire Tae Kwon-Do practice is done without making contact.

Grand Master Kwon, Jae-Hwa, founder of the International Tae Kwon-Do Center, has been teaching martial arts for fifty years. His remarkable strength and youthfulness make the fact of his age seem impossible. With bare hands he can break a rock in two! Humility keeps him from revealing too much about himself, yet people make the pilgrimage from around the world to study with this master.

Practicing Tae Kwon-Do builds strength in body and mind. This fact becomes obvious when you watch students line up and repeat the forms displayed by Master Kwon. The speed, efficiency, power, and concentration in the repetition of a single movement leave no doubt about the capacity of this practice to transform. The natural result of focused practice is a body and mind in perfect harmony. This energy allows the spirit to rise.

Master Kwon says, "When you come into class from the busyness of your life, you forget everything. There is no time for distraction, no choice but to concentrate so you can catch the constantly changing movements." But if the practice stays on a purely physical or mental level, it will not transform you. Tae Kwon-Do is a lifestyle. Honesty, humility, respect, and self-control mark a truly disciplined martial artist.

Master Kwon is a living model of these truths. His humility inspires. Instead of growing old in your striving, you can follow the way of Master Kwon's spirit, and get younger and younger.

36 West 13th Street
bet. 5th & 6th Avenues
New York, NY 10011
Phone: 212-255-8222

Jivamukti Yoga Center

The rapture of yoga

Jivamukti Yoga Center is a feast for the senses. Designed in shades of purple and blue, this 9,000 square foot loft incorporates elements of a traditional temple: enormous murals depicting magical scenes from the East adorn its walls; an indoor waterfall continuously flows into a tiled basin of lotus flowers; and the subtle fragrance of incense carries you through to the Center's practice rooms. The simple meditation hut beckons, always quiet, always open.

Jivamukti Yoga Center is a school and a community. Founded by Sharon Gannon and David Life—an intense, mystical pair with a fierce, grounded passion for yoga—the center has become a spiritual hub, blending Hinduism and Eastern philosophical traditions with elements of hip downtown culture.

The name of the Center, "Jivamukti," means liberation from separation. A beloved yogi once said, "The study of yoga philosophy without a longing for liberation is like dressing up a corpse." Jivamukti Yoga Center is the land of the living. Here, liberation is the ultimate focus of yoga's labors. But freedom doesn't come easy—Jivamukti's yoga classes will push you to your outer physical and mental limits. In a room full of fellow yogis lined up mat to mat, you will be infused with energy. But this is not a yoga competition or a compare-and-despair contest, as the teachers will remind you. The pace of the classes leaves no time for self-pity. The rigorous flowing style challenges you to shed distractions and focus intently on the breath. This focus is the Jivamukti path to freedom.

One form of weekly Jivamukti worship guaranteed to make your spirit soar (rather than making your body sore) is the Monday evening "Kirtan"—a chanting led by devotees of vibrational sound. Don't underestimate the rejuvenating value of two hours of chanting in your search for spiritual nourishment. Here you can join the hundreds of people that gather to sing devotional songs praising the names of God: Shiva-Krishna-Kali-Durga-Lakshmi-Saraswati. Intoning all of God's different faces and forms, this is the "yoga of sound."

Hear the waterfall. Smell the incense. Touch the cool wood floor. See the candles burn. Taste the fruits of yoga practice. Jivamukti liberates without leaving the senses behind.

404 Lafayette Street
bet. 4th Street and Astor Place
New York, NY 10003
Phone: 212-353-0214
www.jivamuktiyoga.com

Kabbalah Center

Mystical Jewish wisdom unveiled

Rabbi Yehuda Grundman of the Kabbalah Center says, "I don't measure a person's spirituality by how much they pray. I judge a person's spirituality by how they act in a traffic jam on a 90-degree day, when their air conditioning is broken and they're late for the most important appointment of their life. In that moment, how do they react to the world?"

If this is the true test of spirituality, we New Yorkers are put to the test every day. In fact, studying the Kabbalah, the ancient wisdom of Jewish mysticism, can teach you how to control and understand many of your reactions to the world—including anger. When you begin to excise the energy that fuels emotionally charged patterns, a new sense of the world's possibilities become available to you.

The teachings of the Kabbalah originate from the Zohar, which is described as a user's manual to the Torah. The Zohar gives instructions for accessing the wisdom and power of the Torah's stories. It also prophesizes that a time will come when people begin to ask deep and provocative questions about the nature of life. It predicted that this inquiry would transform the world into a spiritual place. According to the Zohar, that time is upon us now.

Through lecture, discussion, and a form of meditation that involves passing your eyes over Hebrew letters to absorb their energy (known as "scanning the Zohar"), you begin to distinguish between a life that is merely physical and one that is spiritual. The spiritual life is not something that lies beyond, it lives in "the moment in front of you." You are taking care of yourself and others when you are able to see clearly what is truly needed in this moment; the present moment will take care of all the rest.

The study of the Kabbalah is open to all regardless of faith. At the Kabbalah Center, you can dabble or dive into ancient wisdom and mystical secrets, not the least of which is the secret to finding perfect peace in a traffic jam.

155 East 48th Street
bet. 3rd & Lexington Avenues
New York, NY 10017
Phone: 212-644-0025
www.kabbalah.com

Kelly's Temple

Harlem's most rousing gospel gathering

Sunday at Kelly's Temple is a time and a place to make joyful noise. The drummer lays down a beat; the sound of the organ floods the room; gospel voices call and respond; tambourines shake, hands clap, children stomp, and the congregation rolls, inciting a mighty wave that rocks you from your seat, and makes you tremble with, yes, the Holy Spirit!

This Pentecostal Church on a beaten down block in East Harlem is the quintessential, voices-to-the-rafters gospel gathering. Praise resounds so loudly at Kelly's Temple that, if God chose one place to visit each week, he would surely show up here. You will feel like an honored guest as a smiling usher guides you to your seat, the woman next to you offers to share her Bible, and a lector assures you that "you will be renewed at this service." This world-renowned congregation is famous for its hospitality. Tour buses come around every Sunday to hear Harlem's finest gospel choir. But this service is not a show for tourists; this is 100 percent authentic faith, pure in its love of God and in its belief that God's presence will save us.

During the praise and worship portion of the service, you might be singing "Yes!" over and over again with a conviction that you've never felt before. You could find yourself bellowing out the reassuring lyric, "Don't be discouraged, God is going to show up with healing for your sorrow, healing for your pain, healing for your spirit, giving shelter from the rain." Joining all voices, this incantation needs no answer. The song itself carries its message straight to your heart.

If you're still standing two hours later, you just may witness the baptismal service. Surrendering to the will of God in this congregation doesn't mean dipping one toe or dabbing one finger in the holy water. Surrender is a full-on affair. Baptismal candidates, robed and toweled, go all the way, held by the bishop's strong arms. Don't be afraid, no one is going to try to dunk you in the water. But take warning—it's hard to witness devotion doled out in buckets, if you're measuring your own faith by the teaspoon.

If you've never felt your spirit resurrected, head uptown to Harlem on a Sunday morning. At Kelly's Temple, you can't hide from the weekly reminder that your spirit is alive—shaking, singing, and rejoicing.

8-10-12 East 130th Street
bet. Madison & 5th Avenues
New York, NY 10037
Phone: 212-289-9618

Labyrinth Walks

Step onto the path of tranquility

The whole world knows that New Yorkers are serious walkers. We walk fast and furiously—for exercise and to get where we're going. Recently, interest in reducing stress and deepening consciousness has led some of us to use our well-honed walking skills for a "higher" purpose. We've rediscovered an ancient tool to help us relax, unwind, and regain perspective: the labyrinth.

A labyrinth is an ancient design based on a circle—the universal symbol for unity and wholeness. One concentric line leads from a starting point to the center and back out. It is a meandering passageway with a clear path. Unlike a maze, a labyrinth is not designed to puzzle or confuse. Simply follow the path as it wraps and winds, and it will take you on a journey.

Did you know that the simple act of walking can be an effective meditation? It's a way to calm and center yourself, a way to retune body, mind, and spirit—provided you forget about destination and simply walk. A labyrinth is a tool for walking meditation, encouraging you to bring mind and breath into step.

At the indoor labyrinth at Judson Church, the serene sounds of ancient chants and the soft candlelight create a tranquil environment. The instructions are simple: first, remove your shoes in order to tread lightly on the canvas path; then discover there is no right or wrong way to do a labyrinth walk. Experiment with your pace, method, and movement. Take as much or as little time as you want. Finally, out of respect for yourself and others, observe silence.

Winding around the circle, spiraling toward the center, you begin to unwind internally—stress and anxiety begin to loosen their hold. This simple act of walking calmly and deliberately brings you solidly into your body and closer to the moment-to-moment activity of your mind. The effect? Tranquility. You can create your own labyrinth through city streets. Walking consciously is always an option because it turns out that walking is a strangely radical way to find intimacy with yourself.

Judson Memorial Church
55 Washington Square
bet. Thompson & Sullivan Streets
New York, NY 10011
Phone: 212-477-0351

Laughter Meditation

The city's silliest soulwork

Laraaji, a.k.a. Sir Laughsalot, is a self-described "laugh-master and cosmic musician," who claims that his morning meditation involves closing his eyes and laughing for fifteen minutes straight. Laughter, says this guru of giggles, is a doorway to relaxation and worry-free living.

Laraaji has spent the past twenty years working with laughter as a tool for self-awareness, self-observation, and self-study. His laughter meditation workshops, held all around the city, are an open invitation to explore your spontaneous, playful nature. Self-willed laughter—meaning you're not laughing at someone or something but instead letting laughter erupt from within—can be a way to shake yourself free from worry, anxiety, and stress.

Perhaps the most famous proponent of laughter as powerful mind-body medicine was Norman Cousins, the former editor of the *Saturday Review*. In his best-selling book *Anatomy of an Illness*, Cousins chronicled his battle with a life-threatening connective tissue disease using Vitamin C and megadoses of laughter. He would watch hours of *Candid Camera* television shows and Marx Brothers movies, later writing that "ten minutes of genuine belly laughter had an anesthetic effect and would give me two hours of pain-free sleep." Cousins eventually made a complete recovery.

What Cousins's recovery suggests, and Laraaji instinctively knows, is that laughing oxygenates cells and releases increased levels of endorphins that boost your immune system as well as your mood. It seems that a laughing fit a day not only feels good, it can keep the doctor away.

Laraaji is a master of teaching serious people how to let go and laugh. His workshops begin with chanting and hand drumming as a way to focus the group. As the chanting progresses, Laraaji emits an occasional chuckle. He calls, you respond. At the start, you may feel a bit tight and self-conscious, but sound sends a vibration through your body that warms you up.

Eventually, the chanting evolves into snickers. Then Laraaji lets out a belly-roll. Feeding off his laughter, unsure if you are reacting to this blissed-out man in orange or the hilarity of the situation, you hear yourself erupt with deeper chortles. Fifteen minutes later the entire room is exploding with gales of laughter and, despite yourself, you're at the center of it all.

Working with Laraaji, you might experience what philosopher Rudolf Steiner called "laughter dismantling the ego." You might laugh without inhibition for the first time. You might even learn to laugh like your life depended on it.

Marble Collegiate Church

The birthplace of positive thinking

Dr. Norman Vincent Peale was one of the great spiritual warriors of the 20th century. Energetic, enthusiastic, indefatigable, he would not let negative attitudes shake his faith in God's healing presence. For more than 50 years of Sundays, his booming voice rained down from the pulpit of Marble Collegiate Church with its extraordinary capacity to restore faith and inspire people with a sense that they, too, could confidently draw upon a Higher Power.

Maybe you've read Dr. Peale's inspirational messages in his best-selling book *The Power of Positive Thinking*. Written in 1952, this granddaddy of self-help books is considered by many to have launched the genre. What makes it so special is that it reflects Dr. Peale's keen understanding of psychology and its intimate relationship with spirituality.

Dr. Peale would quote contemporary psychologists as often and as knowledgeably as he would the Bible. He was one of the first to speak about positive visualizations and their profound impact on the mind, and he would frequently draw insightful comparisons between traditional prayer practice and Eastern-type meditation. He was an original "New Ager" but with both feet firmly planted in his Christian faith.

The pioneering work of Dr. Peale continues at Marble Collegiate almost a decade after his death. Called "America's Hometown Church," Marble opens its doors wide to people of every faith, ethnicity, race, and sexual orientation. Minister Peale's successor, Dr. Arthur Caliandro, has forged his own brand of rousing Sunday morning motivational sermons—moving, memorable talks that will cut through your complacency. His homilies are book-ended by glorious, spine-tingling choir songs.

But Marble is no mere Sunday wonder. Almost every evening, it offers spiritual enrichment programs that bring speakers like Dr. Bernie Siegel, writer Anna Quindlen, and *The Artist's Way* author Julia Cameron to the church. And now Marble has created the New Spirit Café in a nearby storefront. Designed primarily for young people, this gathering place offers an upbeat alternative home for those who'd never step foot in a church. With seminar rooms, a bookstore, a coffee and juice bar and cozy conversation nooks, the New Spirit Café is a stimulating place to share cool stories about spiritual synchronicities without ever having to wear your Sunday best.

1 West 29th Street at 5th Avenue
New York, NY 10001-4596
Phone: 212-686-2770
www.marblechurch.org

Mentoring Partnership
of New York

Share your greatest gifts

Was there someone who made a difference in your life when you were growing up? Someone whose presence helped you overcome obstacles and fears—an aunt or an uncle, perhaps, who taught you about discipline, responsibility, confidence, and perseverance, merely by example? Maybe you've heard yourself say, "I wouldn't be where I am today if it wasn't for that one influential person."

These people helped give shape to your character and your future by caring, which is at the heart of mentoring. According to the Mentoring Partnership, "A mentor is a wise and trusted counselor, a teacher—someone who wants to help young people bring out strengths that are already there."

What does all this have to do with keeping your spirit alive? Simple. Give just one person the ability to imagine a future full of hope and possibility, and you'll forever be holding hands with angels.

The Mentoring Partnership of New York is a non-profit organization that works to connect adults with young people who need and want guidance. At orientation sessions, staff members suggest ways to build and strengthen your working relationship with your mentee. Their interactive web site keeps you updated with news, tips, ideas, and inspiring profiles of other mentors.

You're probably qualified to be a mentor right now. Your training is your life. Your commitment is to being a good listener, setting aside a little time regularly, making a new friend. Your reward is the satisfaction of teaching another, of helping shape one link in a chain that will create the future.

The American poet and men's movement leader Robert Bly has said that if young people aren't being actively admired, they're being actively abused. That's heavy stuff. And it magnifies the importance of mentoring. When you offer admiration and praise, when you give the best pieces of yourself to a young person, you can help put a vulnerable life back on course.

Teenagers need good mentors to guide them through the tough years of adolescence and the intensity of growing up in a city rich with temptation. New York City parents need more positive role models for their children. Ironically, it's hard to tell who benefits most from a mentoring partnership—the young person, their parents, or the mentor. In this relationship, everyone wins.

122 East 42nd Street, suite 1520,
at Lexington Avenue
New York, NY 10168
Phone: 212-953-0945/www.mentoring.org

Metropolitan Community Church

God's love delivered judgment-free

Many of us have lost touch with the religious institutions in which we were raised. Many gay, lesbian, and transgender individuals find themselves unwelcome in their original communities of worship. Even so, religion may still inform a sense of identity and view of the world.

Metropolitan Community Church (MCC) is the fastest growing religious organization in the country. It offers refuge to those rejected by the traditional religious organizations simply because of who they are. MCC is a worldwide, inclusive, Christian denomination open to all people, regardless of sexual orientation or lifestyle.

The practices of this church affirm—with scriptural study and scholarly proof—that God is not judging or damning. God's love is for everyone and not just a chosen few. Here, you can finally say goodbye to those Bible-wielding preachers screaming that you're going to hell. At MCC, you will find acceptance, affirmation, and a place for worship. One woman, who began attending services because she wanted to support her best friend, called it the most loving Christian community she had ever found.

Sunday worship services include choir and congregational singing, scriptures, prayers, sermons, and sacraments. Services are brimming with a spirit of inclusiveness and give all members of the congregation the opportunity to express themselves and their love. There is no hiding here, no guilt, no apologies. This is a place where you can raise your voice and rejoice with the knowledge that a Higher Love exists, and it doesn't care who you slept with last night.

Reverend Pat Bumgardner's empowering sermons reflect on passages from the Bible in a way that make parables more relevant today than ever. She explains how Jesus' strength and faith allowed him to confront and challenge the world order to meet the needs of ordinary people. She continually brings that example back to our lives today, and to people who are marginalized and overlooked by public opinion and policy makers. At MCC, you learn that no one can separate you from your inherent goodness or from God.

Want to know that you belong, that you can connect again with a community of worshippers, that you can bow your head but not in shame? Then MCC is the perfect place for a spiritual outing.

446 West 36th Street
bet. 9th & 10th Avenues
New York, NY 10018
Phone: 212-629-7440
www.nycnet.com/mccny

Metropolitan Museum of Art

A gathering of the Gods on Fifth Avenue

If a hard-hearted sixteen-year-old can have his armor cracked by the power of the Met, so can you. Once, trailing behind his class after sketching masks of Oceanic deities, a teenager said he now knew where to go when he needed to be alone. He would hide among the relics, find something to admire, and sit with them until his heart calmed.

Art, it has been said, is the mother of all religions. If it's true, then here in New York we honor the mother like nowhere else on earth—and above all, in our famed Metropolitan Museum of Art. The incredible Met is a massive, monumental shrine to virtually every religion and spiritual tradition in every corner of the planet throughout history. Endless representations of God exist here—from Christ to Krishna, Apollo to Ra, the Buddha to countless African deities. This is truly a house of all gods, unmitigated by a voice from the pulpit.

What that enlightened teenager discovered is a truth available to all visitors who walk through the Met's mighty halls: the weight of history's largest and most diverse collection of artistic works, spread magically through labyrinthine rooms, is heavy enough to cause a stir, or to quiet one within you.

At the Metropolitan Museum you will be awed, and that is the essence of any spiritual journey. No matter your age, the Met's astoundingly diverse collections inspire reverence—even the youngest among us seem to understand that behind each pillared door is a treasure that transcends time and place.

Whether you marvel at the finest detail in a Chinese landscape painting, stand mesmerized at the mystery of the Egyptian sarcophagi, or lose yourself in a meticulously crafted totem from a lost tribe, this is a place to be carried away by creation. It's also a heck of a good place to pray—among this pantheon of gods, somebody's bound to be listening.

1000 Fifth Avenue at 82nd Street
New York, NY 10028
Phone: 212-535-7710

Mount Manresa
Jesuit Retreat Center

Reclaim, restore, renew…RETREAT

A retreat is exactly that—a place to get away from the crowds, from the pressure and pace of your work, from the cyclone spin of your mind. Retreats are not adventure vacations, they are slow times, designed to give you a chance to rest and replenish your energy, to pay attention to your deepest concerns, and to reconnect with yourself and the spirit that moves you.

We all experience the need and desire to escape, to change the scenery of our lives and to reflect on life. We need some unstructured time and uninterrupted tranquility. The question is whether or not you will give yourself such a gift.

Mount Manresa Jesuit Retreat Center, the oldest retreat center in the country, is just a Staten Island Ferry ride away. Nine acres of extraordinary grounds house simple accommodations and dining facilities, a beautiful small chapel, a meditation garden, a library, and scattered shrines tucked between trees and on hilltops placed for far-off views of the city. And that is how the city will feel here—far off.

Unlike the expensive spa escapes that have become trendy and popular today, Mount Manresa is a humble, unpretentious place. The staff won't intrude and won't proselytize (there's no conversion quota here). You're free to structure your day as you wish. But, if you're interested, Father John Ryan, the energetic, extremely loving, and progressive priest who runs the place, will take you on a humor-laced tour of the grounds, complete with esoteric histories and fascinating myths. His warmth is characteristic of Mount Manresa—a place waiting to comfort you, to melt you with its care, to envelop you in un-New York attitude. And it's literally minutes away.

A retreat week or weekend here is affordable and Mount Manresa programs reach out to embrace people in recovery, people with illnesses, seekers from all religious and spiritual denominations, even children and senior citizens. You can attend an organized program or follow a personal path and create your own retreat. Daily meetings offer the support of a respectful staff, while the balance of your time can be spent alone relaxing, reading, thinking, or praying.

Time set aside for contemplation widens and deepens any spiritual path. A retreat is just that—a reprieve from the all-too-familiar ways you can lose yourself in daily routine. A Mount Manresa retreat is a unique opportunity to pamper your neglected soul.

239 Fingerboard Road
Staten Island, NY 10305
Phone: 718-727-3844
www.cptryon.org/manresa
www.maresasi.com

Moving Center-
Gabrielle Roth

Dance and live deeper

If you tell Gabrielle Roth you can't dance, you'd better have better reasons than these: It's too late, I'm too old to start. She'll tell you it is never too late to find your flow. I have no rhythm, no sense of timing. Movement is the nature of the universe. You breathe, you eat, you walk, you even talk in time. Just go with it, she'll reply. I don't have the energy to dance. It takes more energy to suppress movement than it does to surrender to it, she'll say. I've got too much on my mind. She'll tell you to dance with it—when your heart is pumping, your breath is deep, and your mind is clear, answers you've been searching for are suddenly accessible. I don't know the right steps. You were born knowing, she'll insist.

In the more than 30 years that she has been teaching people just like you to move with freedom, fluidity, and grace, Roth has heard all the excuses and has a ready rebuttal for each. When she speaks, she's all down-to-earth practical New Yorker with a demeanor that comforts, and a sense of humor that amuses. Once the tribal rhythms and chants begin and she starts moving, Roth is transformed into a Divine Spirit-Goddess-Shaman-Whirling Dervish.

Roth believes that energy moves in waves, waves move in patterns, patterns move in rhythms, and that we are just that—energy, waves, patterns, rhythms. Dance is her spiritual path. Roth's own experience testifies that you can dance your way through anger, sadness, regret, and frustration and be carried to a sense of your true Self—the sacred Self. World renowned, her workshops reunite the flesh and the spirit, the sensual and soulful.

As a teacher, Gabrielle Roth is an inspiring and seductive guide. She won't teach you how to dance. She's not interested in steps, positions, or pliés. Instead, she will coax your spirit back into your body, and give you permission to let spirit guide you. Under Roth's tutelage, the self-conscious, judging, comparing, fearful mind and shameful body are ordered to listen, learn, and follow an unbounded and powerful inner force as the rhythm of this trance-dance becomes staccato. Your heart pounds in your chest. Your breath is on fire. Your body feels lighter, moving in search of empty spaces.

Roth teaches that breath is the difference between life and death. The deeper you dance, the deeper you breathe, the deeper you live. To dance is to live life in the here-and-now and to the fullest. Gabrielle Roth will take you to a place of personal magic—but you'll have to dance with her to get there.

Phone: 212-769-1381
www.gabrielleroth.com

New York Haiku-kai

A taste of heaven in seventeen syllables

Remember learning haiku—that oddly sparse poetry form—in school? Three lines in a five-seven-five syllabic pattern. Remember taking words apart and fitting them together? Haiku originated as the first verse of a long Japanese poem that was a conversation between poets. What you may not have been taught in school is that writing haiku is playful; it is a social art. A haiku can be a gift to a friend, a form of poetic communication, a way to capture and illuminate the extraordinary moments hiding every-where around you (are you paying enough attention to notice them?).

One small community of New Yorkers has revived this ancient art form and made this writing practice part of their lives. In the Japanese tradition, the New York Haiku-kai is a monthly meeting—a gathering of poets sharing their poems—and a great place to begin your haiku practice.

At the Haiku Society meetings, each poet anonymously submits at least one poem written on an index card. The poems are shuffled together and then read aloud several times by the evening's designated reader. After the few words are spoken, there is a pregnant quiet that takes you on the poem's journey. All the poets lis-ten for key words and phrases that hold grace for them. The members then go around and share what struck them in their five favorite poems. All the while, the authors remain discretely unknown. Through this act of listening and the exchange that follows, you can learn to write a provocative haiku and feel how the real spirit of haiku brings tiny moments to life.

This practice is completely portable; it goes wherever you go. All you need is a pen, a small scrap of paper (even a taxi receipt will do), agile fingers, and an open heart and mind to be a haiku traveler. Haiku writing requires no preparation—in fact, the form urges you to exercise a kind of spontaneous flexibility.

Writing haiku connects you to people, to the season, and to the present. You will not be alone when you notice

little leaves bursting

everywhere spring's bright green haze

shimmers in the trees

And doubtless, you will discover in your lines what is abundant in our city—ripe moments of urban humanity.

Anticipating the monthly Haiku-kai meeting, you might find yourself haiku-ing your way around the city, fingers flickering to count syllables. This act of writing brings you closer to life and its details.

New York Insight Meditation

Inhale, exhale, and calm will prevail

Every human on earth shares something in common: we breathe. Breath is the unbroken chain that carries us through life. It is our most faithful companion, but many of us go through an entire lifetime unaware of our breath.

The simple meditation instructions you receive at a New York Insight (NYI) sitting will gently direct your attention to the sensations of breathing. Insight Meditation, also known as Vipassana Buddhism, focuses on cultivating mindfulness—a non-judgmental presence of mind achieved by using the breath as the object of attention. From here, many practitioners believe an expansive understanding of self and of soul are possible.

Attending a New York Insight Meditation sitting is a reminder to be awake to your breathing. These gatherings—which take place at various locations throughout the city—are relaxed, with participants of all ages, backgrounds, and experience. Short sitting and walking meditations are followed by inspiring readings, discussion, and time for questions. Facilitators rely less on rigid teachings and more on personal experience in leading the meditation, making this practice welcoming and comfortable.

During the group discussion, you can talk about the challenges of focusing and concentrating your mind. Meditation is truly an art that requires practice and the willingness to begin over and over again. But, like riding a bike or playing an instrument, when it's learned, it becomes part of you and is not easily forgotten.

At one discussion, a middle-aged man shared a story that seemed to capture the value of Insight Meditation. He left his apartment to run errands one evening. But rather than descending smoothly, the elevator gave a few quirky jolts and suddenly stopped. Immediately his mind started to race. He cursed the "incompetent" building superintendent, he cursed the "negligent" building owner, he even cursed the "sabotaging" universe for inconveniencing him.

Then he remembered his breath. He was amazed at how shallow his breathing had become, how constricted his chest felt. He began to watch his breath—at first, small and tight—slowly grow deeper, steadier, smoother. His mind began to quiet and release its angry thoughts. He sat down on the floor and continued to breathe mindfully for the next 20 minutes. When he finally reached the lobby he was not agitated and irritable but actually calm.

Insight Meditation does not require special props or seats and can be practiced anywhere. If you're breathing (are you?), you're ready.

P.O. Box 1790, Murray Hill Station
New York, NY 10156
Phone: 917-441-0915
www.nyimc.org

New York Open Center

Epicenter of spiritual learning

When we confine ourselves to the comfortable, to the safe and small, we limit our opportunities for peak experiences and personal expansion. Our souls may feel secure, but they will never soar.

At the New York Open Center, you'll find hundreds of ways to energize and challenge the spirit. Because secular education often neglects the soul, this center for holistic learning has dedicated itself to helping people test limits, take risks, and explore the edges of convention. Here, a diverse, spiritually based program of workshops, seminars, and wellness services promote connection, discovery and, if necessary, recovery.

If you find yourself stagnant, your senses dulled by the daily grind, a class at the Open Center can change the trajectory of your thinking. Whether you sign up for African Dance, Asian Health Secrets, Jewish Mysticism, or the Conference on the Art of Dying, the Center's goal is to help you make connections between your intellect and your emotions, your spirit and your body. These kinds of connections—borne out of a desire for continued personal growth—promise to add new dimension to a life lived narrowly.

In its 20 years, the Open Center has pioneered programs on the world's spiritual traditions and has become an oasis for those who take spiritual inquiry seriously. You can participate in long term study of Buddhism, Christianity, Mysticism, Kabbalah, Sufism, Taoism, or Shamanism. Or you can participate in a one-day workshop on esoteric subjects such as Santeria, Qi Gong, mandala painting, or the Alexander Technique.

What's most remarkable about the Open Center is how accessible the courses are. This is not a school of "enlightened" experts intent on hearing their own voices. The Center exists more as a holistic laboratory, a place where new ideas are respected, unique approaches to awareness are considered, and fresh avenues for creativity and expression are embraced and taught by perceptive and original thinkers.

Take a risk. Take a leap. Take a class. The door is always open.

83 Spring Street
bet. Broadway and Lafayette Street
New York, NY 10012
Phone: 212-219-2527
www.opencenter.org

92nd Street Y

Where the mind never stops learning

Picture your spirit. Is the image you see ageless, radiant with energy, curious and playful, inquisitive, eager for knowledge, enthusiastic, and free?

These are the qualities at the core of every human spirit, and when they're nurtured and fed, life shimmers with added meaning and joy. The 92nd Street Y offers programs which sustain us mentally and physically, keeping the inquisitive child in us (you can substitute "child" for "spirit" any time you wish) stimulated and happy. At the Y you can put your mind to work, your body to play, your hands to create, your voice to debate, your feet to tour, your heart to pray—and you can do it every day.

Look through the Y's catalog. No stone is left unturned when it comes to a sheer, unbounded delight in learning; it's a one-stop shop for complete personal enrichment. The Y's mission is to invigorate and stimulate all who pass through its doors, and to create programs of interest for people of every age. In terms of energy, excitement, and infinite options, the Y is a microcosm of the city. Here, visitors from age 8 to 80 move like freshmen on a college campus, delighting in the possibilities.

The year 2000 marked the 92nd Street Y's 125th anniversary. Founded by visionary Jewish leaders, the Y has always offered a wealth of courses focusing on New York's unique history and eccentricities. Frequent city tours place you in the center of fascinating ethnic neighborhoods in the presence of magnificent architecture. And now the Y has stretched its borders considerably, hosting cultural excursions to a re-emerging Cuba and remote parts of Tibet and Bhutan, among many other fascinating destinations.

Maybe you know the Y because of its sensational children's parties or because you've committed to a regimen of exercise in a class or at the pool. Or perhaps you've attended the Y's renowned lecture and reading series, or its poetry center, which attracts a line-up of the most revered and controversial thinkers, writers, and poets to its stage. You will be amazed that these luminaries agree to be your teachers, even for a night. Such is the drawing power of the 92nd St. Y.

Expect your mind to return to its original sponge-like nature when you pour yourself into the Y's unlimited programming. The Y is founded on the premise that the passion to learn doesn't fade with age but continues to grow even deeper. We are born with enthusiasm, with our batteries fully charged. The 92nd Street Y keeps you plugged in and energized.

1395 Lexington Avenue
bet. 92nd & 93rd Streets
New York, NY 10128
Phone: 212-996-1100
www.92ndsty.org

Noonday
Concert Series

Squeeze some harmony into your lunch hour

Guiseppe Mazzini called music "the harmonious voice of creation, an echo of the invisible world." The invisible lives inside you, and calling it forth with the sounds of music can be a powerful way to nourish the spirit—especially when you can fit it in during your lunch hour.

Like many of the city's churches, chapels, and temples, these lower Manhattan landmarks have sought ways to fill their seats beyond the traditional Sunday services. The Noonday Concert Series draws a mixed crowd to St. Paul's on Mondays and to Trinity on Thursdays for ecumenical celebrations. These lunch hour congregations come together simply to hear string quartets and accomplished ensembles play Bach, Beethoven, and Mozart.

While some in the pews use this background of sublime sound to balance checkbooks or tackle the *New York Times* crossword puzzle, the real gift of the music lies in actively engaging with it, being conscious of the calming effect it has on a distracted mind. The balcony offers a fine elevated view of the performers or a perfect place to close the eyes and be swept away by each transcendent note. Just this simple act of truly paying attention to the flow of the music is a form of useful meditation that can ease you through the balance of your work day. Regardless of how you choose to experience the Noonday Concert Series, the music is a soothing antidote to the sensory assault of subways, cell phones, and shrillness in the street.

On the wall of St. Paul's Chapel, above George Washington's pew, hangs an original casting of the Great Seal of the United States, proclaiming E Pluribus Unum—"from many, we are one." In the 200 years since the Great Seal was commissioned, the ethnic, cultural, and religious mix of New York has grown more diverse. Music continues to be our universal language and a common source of rapture.

St. Paul's Church
Broadway at Fulton Street
Trinity Church, Broadway at Wall Street
212-602-0747
Concert Calendar Hotline:
www.trinitywallstreet.org

Poets House

☆

Uplift the human spirit through poetry

If God really is in the details, then poets have a head start on the way to enlightenment. A poet is aware of the world, sensitive to small things. This ability to contemplate life's subtle details is connected to the development of a "spiritual eye"—the power to see truth.

The atmosphere at Poets House inspires contemplation and creation and offers the best of both worlds—all the poetry you would want to read in a lifetime and the perfect environment in which to do it. The poetry collection is larger than that of the Library of Congress and includes every volume published in the United States since 1990. In this sanctuary, you can experience the power of the word through reading or penning your own poems.

Poets House was founded in 1986 on the belief that poetry "is central to the human spirit." A refuge from the frenetic world outside, here you can sink down into life's deeper questions or journey endlessly into the range of human emotions. Whatever mood you are in—melancholy, angry, exuberant, or nostalgic—you will find a piece of poetry reflecting your emotion. This discovery can illuminate you, release you, change you. Poets House is a source of self-expression bound into 40,000 volumes.

At Poets House, you can also listen to recordings of poets reading their work. If you've ever been to a poetry reading, you know how listening to a poem read aloud can animate the carefully selected words, sending pictures stretching across your imagination. A deliberate inflection in an author's voice can hidden meanings. Poets House contains a newly catalogued collection of remarkable poets in performance, including the voices of e.e. cummings, Elizabeth Bishop, Dylan Thomas, and Gwendolyn Brooks.

Audre Lorde said that poetry is not a luxury, but rather "a bridge across our fears of what has never been before." Poets House may be the longest bridge with the most expansive views in New York.

72 Spring Street, 2nd floor,
bet. Broadway & Lafayette Street
New York, NY 10012
Phone: 212-431-7920
www.poetshouse.org

Religious Society of Friends

Find yourself in a sea of silence

Henry David Thoreau wrote, "Silence is the universal refuge." Intervals of quiet are deeply healing to your spirit, and Quakers, famous for their silent meetings, can teach us much about the art of silence.

Quaker meetings are a source of wisdom, strength, and renewal. There is no minister in this community, no clergy to lead the way through a sermon. According to the Friends, everyone is clergy, capable of and responsible for giving ministry. All of us have equal access to an inner religious experience, to "the Inner Light."

The Sunday Meeting for Worship is central to the Quaker practice; it demonstrates the depth of wisdom that can rise up from a still pool of silence. At the Meeting for Worship, when the silence is broken, you listen clearly to the words being spoken—you understand them. The word "quake" describes the feeling in your body when you break your own silence in response to a call from within. One woman rose at a recent meeting and asked, "How deep is Meeting for Worship? Deep enough to go below our thoughts. How deep is Meeting for Worship? Deep enough to hold every message, deep enough to bind us, deep enough to save us all."

In the Quaker tradition, God is an accessible presence. As you explore your relationship with God, you begin to question your relationship with humanity and consider the shape of your responsibility to the outside world. Peaceful activism is a Quaker trademark. As a matter of conscience, they invest time and energy in political and social causes to protect human rights and promote justice, non-violence, and peace. Of course, you don't have to be an activist to be a Quaker, but engaging with this community may prompt you to act.

Peace and quiet—the cornerstones of the Quaker tradition—have the power to erase your feelings of isolation, and leave you with a sense of gratitude and abundance. This hour, shared in the company of Friends, can become the most sacred 60 minutes of your week.

221 East 15th Street
bet. 2nd & 3rd Avenues
New York, NY 10003
Phone: 212-777-8866
www.metroquakers.org

Riverside Church

Review your life from the top down

You're discouraged, feeling stuck. You've let weeds grow around your dreams, lost sight of your goals. Sounds like you need a change in perspective.

A new view of the world leads to excitement, euphoria, and the urge for adventure—something that's hard to see when our heads are focused on the sidewalk below. For a quick change in perspective visit Riverside Church, where you'll need to drag your feelings of inertia 392 feet above the streets to the panoramic view from the Bell Tower observation deck (don't worry, an elevator covers most of it). Talk about perspective! From this height, even the mighty Hudson looks clean enough to drink.

The enormous Bell Tower holds more than 100 tons of carillon bells. Some bells are as big as elephants and all dangle from the steel girded entrails of the giant sandcastle-like tower. The sound they make—deep, strong, and melodious—will shake you to your foundations when you're in their midst. Some body-centered therapies claim that this kind of "sonic cleansing" can actually clear energy blocks in the body. Want to feel it yourself? You can catch these vibrations every Sunday morning before and after the 10:45 a.m. worship service.

The bell tower is not the only place at Riverside Church that offers a change in perspective; the

Church's Wellness Center focuses on community as a source of healing and recovery, as opposed to pre-scriptions and physicians. The Center also offers extensive bereavement support services to comfort the sick and grieving while providing a spiritual framework in which to understand and cope with loss. The Sunday morning healing service in the Chapel also includes a laying-on-of-hands ceremony—an ancient rite of passage for the sick. Riverside Church is built on a philosophy that "the whole of community is only as strong and viable as the most vulnerable." No one is left uncared for here.

Riverside Church is a place to gain fresh perspective in more ways than one—even if you have to go to the very top floor to get it.

490 Riverside Drive at 120th Street
New York, NY 10027
Phone: 212-870-6700
www.theriversidechurchny.org

Sanctuary Restaurant

Food for the spiritually hungry

Have you ever thought that eating could be a spiritual practice?

It is at the Sanctuary Restaurant. In fact, the people at the Interfaith League of Devotees (a Hindu organization which manages the Sanctuary) believe that the spiritual journey begins with purifying the body and their mission is to uplift the spirit by nourishing—literally—the body that houses it. According to their philosophy, when you consciously eat food that has been prepared with reverence, eating becomes a spiritual practice.

With many of the world's finest restaurants located in this city, New Yorkers know platefuls about worshipping food—but more with an epicure's interest than the fervor of a spiritual seeker. Often we eat on the run, and rarely do we take the time to give thanks for the fruits that fuel us. We're bombarded with information about the effect of diet and nutrition on our physical health but know little about food's effect on our state of mind.

If you think about it, all of the world's religions have culinary caveats—dietary restrictions are imposed, ritual feasts and fasts are observed. For thousands of years, we've been taught that food is sacred. This is certainly the belief at the Sanctuary Restaurant, where all food is "karma free," meaning you pay for it in this lifetime, not in the next.

One essential food-related ritual observed at the Sanctuary is called prasad—the offering of food to God as a sign of devotion. According to Hindu scriptures, food becomes sanctified or purified by offering it up to God. Fruits and vegetables, used later in fresh juices, soups, and salads, adorn the altar in the Krishna Temple above the restaurant; in effect, they are brought before God before they are brought before you. Sanctified foods purify your mind and body, while realigning you with your spirit. Sounds like true "soul food."

At the Sanctuary Restaurant, there are two cooks in house—the human and the divine. The food is simple and strictly vegetarian. The ambience (and the service) is relaxed. If the Hindu concept of prasad is difficult to digest, then forget it. Instead, try the seaweed soup and sip it slowly. It will make you a believer.

Interfaith League of Devotees
25 First Avenue
bet. 1st & 2nd Streets
New York, NY 10002
Phone: 212-473-0370

Statue of Liberty and Ellis Island

Symbols of the quest for freedom

Remembering where we came from helps us see where we're going. A visit to two of New York's classic landmarks is a simple reminder of the noble principles that protect our right to seek spiritual renewal in the first place.

The Statue of Liberty Enlightening the World—as Lady Liberty is officially called—rises up like Venus out of the murky waters of New York Harbor. She is a symbol of the inalienable American right to act, believe, and express your spirit in whatever way you choose. At the time of her unveiling, Lady Liberty was among New York's tallest structures, with her arm raised to the heavens reminding us where to turn for comfort.

Gazing up at the statue's enormous copper skin inspires the same breathtaking amazement you might find at the foot of a sacred mountain. Lady Liberty is indeed colossal, but the height of the ideals she stands for is even more compelling. Inside her iron skeleton, designed by Frenchman Frédéric-Auguste Bartholdi, 500 winding steps lead to amazing vistas. Despite the realities of injustice, greed, hatred, and repression that she witnesses daily, the Statue of Liberty tirelessly stands vigil, challenging us to imagine our potential, what we can become.

Just across the Harbor, Ellis Island is a testament to our nation's immigrant history. Its newly refurbished Immigration Museum tells the story of the greatest wave of incoming humanity in our nation's history. Between 1892 and 1954, some 12 million people fled the poverty, famine, religious persecution, and political unrest of their homelands and made their way to America entering through Ellis Island. You may find your own family's history among the museum's artifacts, photos, maps and records. Oral histories and films tell poignant stories. These moving testimonies not only help you trace your roots, but have to power to bring your own quest for fulfillment into focus.

We come to New York from around the globe—to live, to work, to play, to seek, to find. The Statue of Liberty and Ellis Island are symbols of the freedom we have to explore our lives more fully and freely. A pilgrimage to these landmarks can reawaken our passion to exercise these rights.

The Circle Line Ferry
212-269-5755
www.ellisisland.org

Sufi Books

A mecca for spiritual pilgrims

When Shirley MacLaine wrote about the Bodhi Tree Bookstore in her best-seller *Out On A Limb*, she turned the Los Angeles alternative bookstore into a mecca for New Agers overnight. The Bodhi became a mandatory destination for spiritual tourists on their quest for enlightenment.

New York has its own version of the Bodhi Tree. Sufi Books, located in Tribeca, is one of the East Coast's most comprehensive spiritual bookstores. It specializes in the writings of Sufi masters—including the mystical poets Rumi and Hafiz—as well as the spirituality of Islam. Here you can also browse among the finest selection of books on nearly every religious and spiritual tradition from around the world.

Books are a tremendous source of inspiration and renewal. Find an author whose voice resonates poignantly for you and you'll have an immediate source of insight, solace, and support. When language is imbued with grace, the well-written word can ignite passion and provoke action. Books evoke joy, laughter, love, pain, fear, anger, and compassion—all the emotions that make you more alive.

This gem of a bookstore combines a superior selection of spiritual writings with a meticulous manner of display. Clearly, books are worshipped here. Each shelf is arranged with such reverence and care, you might find that it affects the way you handle the books, the way you savor their words. Sufi Books houses an eternity's worth of spiritual inquiry in a space that looks and feels like a temple honoring the planet's enduring wisdom.

Once you explore the wealth of literature and devotional music, check out Sufi Book's quarterly calendar of events. The readings, classes, and workshops will have you grabbing your date book and reshuffling appointments. When you do, you'll find yourself among a dozen or so inquisitive souls, engaged in nose-to-nose conversation with the author of a book that shaped their lives.

Make Sufi Books your personal launching pad. Open yourself to the many precious, profound, and poetic sources of wisdom, and they will be yours for a lifetime.

227 West Broadway
bet. White & Franklin Streets
New York, NY 10013
Phone: 212-334-5212
www.sufibooks.com

Sweet Honey in the Rock

A cappella divas who rock your soul

"We who believe in freedom cannot rest until it comes." –Sweet Honey in the Rock.

Once you've heard Sweet Honey in the Rock singing lyrics like these, don't be surprised to find yourself at the front of the ticket line to see them again and again. This African–American women's a cappella group is a powerful voice for freedom, justice, and peace. For 26 years they have been weaving their voices together into an instrument of sound that's rooted in the African–American experience. Spirituals, blues, gospel, and traditional African chants are the belly of Sweet Honey's fiery expression.

Sweet Honey is comprised of six women—five voices creating an unbelievable range of sounds, from the sweetest highs to plunging bass depths, and one mesmerizing woman who gestures sign language's rich beauty with her hands. A Sweet Honey concert will stretch, ravish, and make you ache to catch every potent expression. And their message, so powerfully delivered, needs to be heard. Their songs, full of forceful social and political conviction, draw your attention to both the hardship and beauty of life.

Each year, Sweet Honey plays at least twice in the city. At their annual fall concert at Carnegie Hall, the acoustics magnify their musical brilliance and standing ovations erupt in waves. For Martin Luther King Jr.'s birthday in late winter, the group expresses their commitment to children in a more humble setting—the auditorium at Washington Irving High School. If you are looking for a sensational "raise the spiritual roof" outing with the kids, put this event on your calendar. Inevitably, the singing and signing sextet marches through the audience filling the room with exuberance. Kids join them on stage to make music in the spirit of a joy-filled party. At the heart of all of the celebration is Sweet Honey's power to educate, to convey a greater understanding of our nation's history and Dr. King's work. This moment of learning is filled with love and overflows with pride.

Every second of a Sweet Honey in the Rock concert is intended to touch and wake the audience. And it does. As they exit the stage, still singing in the wings, you will find that Sweet Honey's voices and messages linger long after the show comes to its rousing conclusion.

c/o Paula Cole Jones
Administrator
P.O. Box 77442
Washington, D.C. 20013
www.sweethoney.com

The Tarot School

Become a psychic, read your future

Everyone has been tempted by those storefront psychics—gypsy-like women who appear mysteriously in doorways, beckoning to read your palm or your cards. In vulnerable moments, or when we fall hopelessly off our paths, tarot readers, psychics and clairvoyants may offer reassurance, validation, even revelations that seem to illuminate our futures. These fascinating, often gifted "seers" possess a knowledge and sensitivity that you too can develop.

Today, tarot card readings are a particularly popular approach to self-inquiry. At the Tarot School, you'll learn how to read tarot cards for yourself and for others. Reading the tarot will teach you clarity about yourself, your emotional issues, your spiritual direction, your past and your future.

At both the Monday night classes and the correspondence courses, all 78 cards of the deck are closely studied and their hidden meanings exposed. During the hands-on portion of the class, you hone your skills to interpret the cards' messages. The true magic of the tarot is that, regardless of your experience or your esoteric knowledge, you can use them immediately. With their rich illustrations, the cards hold the power to bring your life's purpose into clearer focus. Wald Amberstone, a Certified Tarot Grand Master and teacher at the Tarot School, says, "Through the tarot you can pursue and capture the unicorn of your own inner form, which you only dimly see every once in a while through the forest of everyday life."

The tarot has a long heritage, originating in Northern Italy in the mid-1400s and used by nobility as an educational game. Over the next 500 years, tarot reading evolved into a tradition of magic and esotericism. The tarot is another language built on pictures. Its meaning taken from Medieval and Renaissance cultures, the cards blend alchemy, kabbalah, numerology, theosophy, and astrology.

Amberstone says, "Carrying the tarot is like carrying around your own portable inner space. It is a mystical hole in your pocket. You can take out the cards, pull one, and jump through a hole in your spirit to another place." You don't know where this leap will take you because you pick by chance. Yet interpreting the card that has fallen before you will point you where you need to go.

Classes held at the Source of Life Center
22 West 34th Street 5th floor,
bet. 5th & 6th Avenues
New York, NY 10001
Phone: (800) 804-2184
www.TarotSchool.com

Terry Schreiber Studio

Play the leading role in your own discovery

Terry Schreiber says that acting begins for many as an escape from their lives, but eventually it becomes a journey to truth. It requires the courage to stand emotionally naked, open and vulnerable. Acting, he concludes, demands dedication of mind, heart, and will.

The halls of the T. Schreiber Studio are sprinkled with pensive, pacing actors getting into character, rehearsing their lines. The craft as taught and practiced here calls for the actor to clear out emotional baggage and explore new concepts of the Self. In every corner of the studio students and teachers attempt to shed old skins and let go of inhibitions.

Classes start with mind-body exercises ranging from meditation and Pilates (a stretching and strengthening discipline that elongates and opens the body) to bioenergetics (body-centered exercises designed to remove emotional energy blocks). Relaxation and concentration of mind are established, and then the work (or play) moves toward activating imagination.

One teacher here described acting as a fantastic exploration of the body. At the T. Schreiber Studio, the body and the senses are considered portals to the creative life of the student. Passing through these doorways is a sacred journey.

The Studio's classes and workshops invite both beginners and working professionals to surrender the ego so they can "exercise" their souls. There is no doubt—acting is a spiritual endeavor. It is a chance to be fully alive in the body and use personal history to generate a catharsis of character—to be so much yourself that you can become another.

When acting is defined as this type of inquiry, we are struck by its potential for spiritual discovery. We have to reconsider weathered clichés about New York being a city of actors employed as waiters; in fact, this may be a city of courageous seekers waiting for their awakening.

151 W. 26th Street, 7th floor,
bet. 6th & 7th Avenues
New York, NY 10001
Phone: 212-741-0209

Union Square Green Market

●

Root yourself in Mother Earth's abundance

Consider this: the slower, gentler rhythms of nature are calming to body, mind and spirit. Accessing those vibrations, wherever and whenever possible, rejuvenates us. That is the magic of the Green Market, affectionately known as the Farmer's Market—a nourishing, nurturing, life-affirming scene that's repeated around the city several times a week.

New York City's concrete crust can leave you wondering what's happening in the earth below, but the Farmer's Market fills in the blank. Stalls overflow with the season's harvest bringing the land and its bounty closer to home. Your senses feast upon a rainbow of vibrant colors—golden peppers, crimson beets, rich red apples plucked from the tree just hours before—along with the reassuring fragrance of the soil carried on the backs of carrots, onions, potatoes, and squash.

Your mind responds, your appetite blossoms, and your body anticipates the wholesome, organic gastronomical adventure to come. It's this ritual that has turned a trip to the Farmer's Market into a true form of worship for many city dwellers.

The Greenmarket organization has been around since 1976, organizing and managing more than two dozen open air farmer's markets throughout New York City. Regional farmers bring their bounty—fruits and vegetables, fish, meat, poultry, eggs, dairy, honey, breads, and flowers—to be sold in designated public markets. All the items must be grown, raised, or produced by the grower and be impeccably fresh.

Shopping at the Farmer's Market breaks the cycle of not knowing the source of your food. It evokes a sense of connection to the earth and to the foods you eat (an awareness that some researchers think can actually enhance a food's nutritional value). This connection, whether you are conscious of it or not, is invigorating, even health inducing. You see the face of the woman who unearthed your radishes and squashes, the arms of the man who pressed your cider, the hands of the growers who picked your beans and aged your cheeses. These farmers bring with them not only their prized harvests but also a reminder of their rural roots and the slower pace of the countryside.

All this freshness simmers in your kitchen, sustains friends and family, and renews you at the most basic and essential level. Regular visits to one of the city's Farmer's Markets is a great way to feed the soul.

East 17th Street at Broadway
Phone: 212-477-3220
Mon., Wed., Fri., Sat., 8 a.m.–6 p.m.
Open Year Round

United Nations Temple of Understanding

A sweeping spiritual tour

Spirituality is good for you. A number of recent studies show that people who believe, who answer "yes" when asked "Are you spiritual?" tend to live longer, healthier lives. It doesn't seem to matter who or what you put your faith in; it's merely important to believe in some form of Higher Power.

The spiritual quest is fundamental to being human, and in New York you can set out on an extraordinary quest indeed. "Spirituality and Different Religious Traditions" is a program co-sponsored by the United Nations Temple of Understanding that takes you on a sweeping spiritual tour of the city one Saturday each month. Over the course of seven months you become immersed in another faith. You will examine the symbols, beliefs, practices, and community life of seven different religious traditions—Hinduism, Jainism, Native American Spirituality, Christianity, Islam, Buddhism, and Judaism.

While visiting the houses of worship, you'll learn about the adornments, art, and architecture of each. You will join in rituals, prayers, and practices during these packed days of spiritual feasting. You'll feel like a privileged guest as you sit down for a meal and conversation with members of the congregation. The UN Program highlights the common ground and the shared visions of all seven religious traditions.

Juliet Hollister, the founder of the UN Temple of Understanding, believes that at heart all of us are spiritual individuals, and that our evolution is a spiritual one. She imagined a place where the people of the world's religions could come together for dialogue and understanding without compromising their own beliefs.

In its forty-year history, the Temple has garnered the support and participation of spiritual and political leaders from every continent, including His Holiness the Dalai Lama, Pope John XXIII, Mother Teresa, Thomas Merton, Nelson Mandela, Albert Schweitzer, Eleanor Roosevelt, and Anwar-el Sadat. With advocates like these, the Temple has survived as one of the oldest global, interfaith, interracial, independent, spiritual organizations in the world.

The Temple of Understanding can't be contained in one single building. Instead, its structure is the houses of worship of all the faiths. The Temple's progressive web site stands as a virtual meeting place for times when you can't roam the corridors of Christianity, the halls of Hinduism, or the mosques of Islam in New York. With just a click you can visit another world of the spirit or pause at the online image of a reflecting pool to cast forth your prayers.

720 Fifth Avenue, 16th floor,
at 56th Street
New York, NY 10019
Phone: 212-246-2746
www.templeofunderstanding.org

Village Zendo

Meditate with a modern-day master

Sensei Pat O'Hara, the founding teacher of Village Zendo, describes her role as a meditator as "finding a lotus in the fire." Her Zen Buddhist meditation center in Greenwich Village is a thousand-petaled wonder, offering a simple path toward peace and well being.

Zen Buddhism took shape when the original teachings of the Buddha migrated east from India and became influenced by the cultures and philosophies of China and Japan. The aesthetics of the meditation practice at Village Zendo are unmistakably Japanese. The objects at the Zendo are meticulously placed, and thoughtful rituals integrated into the practice maintain the Japanese tradition. Bells are rung, chants are sung, and wooden gongs are struck in precise patterns. Participants also perform a series of bows offered as gestures of surrender.

Pat O'Hara greets all newcomers at the door with an embracing friendliness characteristic of everyone at Village Zendo. This warmth, along with individualized instruction for beginners, calm any anxiety you have about Zen Buddhist meditation. In fact, Sensei O'Hara says, "Don't get too devotional, that is not where freedom is to be found," suggesting that a beginner's mind is valued here.

Meditation practice, called zazen in Japanese, is done with eyes open, facing a clean eggshell-colored wall. Pat O'Hara speaks about the courage to face the wall and be with your self. The reverence in her description makes you feel that this mere act of sitting could lead to instant epiphanies. This simplest of exercises takes on momentous importance.

Each week in the Thursday night teaching, Sensei O'Hara lights some incense and talks for the time it takes one fragrant stick to burn down. Keeping with Zen tradition, she tells a story of a meeting between master and student, which culminates in the offering of a koan—a riddle whose words have the power to wake your entire being. To solve the koan, you will have to think with the whole of you—body, mind, and spirit.

At Village Zendo, truths are folded into mysterious word packages, waiting to be opened and read like a palm. The koans could be 1,000 years old, and yet still contain relevant and timely pearls of wisdom. Sensei O'Hara brings a tenderness and stillness to the moment. Her gentleness and the teachings of Zen are waiting to deliver you to the flowering lotus inside.

200 Varick Street
Suite 902
New York, NY 10014
212.340.4656

World Music Institute

Caretaker of the world's most sacred music

Many of the world's music and dance traditions were born as forms of worship—as ways to transcend body and mind. Like stories and myths, indigenous music often defines the sacred beliefs and values of a culture. On a mission to unravel the rich mysteries of music, or perhaps to keep them intact, the World Music Institute (WMI) brings the planet's sacred songs to New York. The WMI is devoted to presenting music and dance forms rooted in the local traditions of cultures all over the world.

Music has historically been a powerful tool for elevating the spirit. Masterpieces such as Bach's liturgical works or the music of Sufi Master Hazrat Inayat Khan are considered by some to be a means of direct communication with God. Devotional music, like the ragas of India or Gregorian chants, can transport the mind and spirit to a sacred realm. All are available for your enrichment in some form at the World Music Institute.

At a WMI concert, where you will share in and experience the ancient sounds of other cultures, your own spirit will join the celebration. When used to express any powerful message—the will of a people, the story of life, reaching out for the Divine—music can effortlessly uplift you with its purposeful sound. In the silence after a song, you may find an exquisite quiet within, a fullness of feeling, rapture, or pieces of your own story revealed through music.

As our nation's largest caretaker of international music, the WMI also has a unique mission to preserve, protect, and perform traditional music endangered by wars, political unrest, or technological obsolescence. Like few experiences you will ever have, the WMI performances enthusiastically celebrate life. Not only through song, but also through costumes and dress, language and stories, ancient instruments, movements, melodies, rhythms and dance. There is an opportunity to find your own ethnic and cultural past in the lament and joy that echoes through the songs of others. Music serves as a great ambassador for our shared human experiences.

All of the performances at the WMI will remind you that wherever you go in the world, joy, love, and exuberance still exist, that people are grateful for life and express that gratitude in song. Music, in all its glorious forms, offers hope.

49 West 27th Street, suite 930,
bet. Broadway & 6th Avenue
New York, NY 10001
Phone: 212-545-7536
www.heartheworld.org

The Spa Experience

Day spas are springing up throughout the city, offering exotic beauty treatments and luxurious programs for pampering the body. Here we've highlighted five spas that go beyond mere manicures, massages, and facials to focus attention on your whole being. Either because of their unique environments, extraordinary practitioners, integrated holistic services, or foundations in spiritual principles, these day spas can lead you to a greater sense of enhanced health and expanded consciousness. A spa retreat that works below the surface to bring body, mind, and soul into alignment is a special gift to the spirit—a way to unlock its energy, restore vitality, and feel truly alive.

Stone Spa

Deep contentment is offered in the form of an ancient healing practice that combines smooth heated stones and therapeutic massage to melt tension from your body. The basalt river rocks are warmed to 125 degrees in a pool of water, then nestled into the small of the back, placed in palms, or guided along the well-oiled muscles of your neck and shoulders.

At the Stone Spa, you'll feel rebalanced by the subtle juxtapositions of the four elements: the grounding density of the earth stones, the fluidity of the warm water, and the fire of candlelight dancing through aromatherapeutic air. Lie back and let out a sigh from deep within your soul.

104 West 14th Street, 2nd Floor
bet. 6th and 7th Avenues
Phone: 212-741-0880

Millefleurs Day Spa

Open until midnight, Millefleurs Day Spa is a Moroccan oasis tucked into Tribeca. Designed in the spirit of a Middle Eastern temple, the space has a light, open "outer court" and private, womb-like "inner chambers." Shifting between the two spaces, you take the journey that Millefleurs' visionary owner intended—to touch the sacred in yourself.

Deep massage, medicinal herbal body wraps, acupuncture treatments, tarot readings, aromatic steam saunas, even decorative henna tattoos (known as Mendhi) are available to renew whatever part of you needs to be touched, adorned, shed, or released. This kind of concentrated pampering is a generous way to bring the spirit back to life.

130 Franklin Street at Varick
New York, NY 10001
Phone: 212-966-3656

El Noël Wellness Center Day Spa

At El Noël Wellness Center and Day Spa, western medicine is seamlessly integrated with other ancient and enduring healing traditions such as shiatsu and Swedish massage, aromatherapy, hatha yoga, and tai chi. El Noël was conceived and achieved by the sibling trio of Dr. Yvonne Noël, a board certified ob/gyn, her brother, Dr. Ruthven Noël, a specialist in internal medicine, and sister, Monica Noël, a massage therapist. Here, self-care is considered more than a luxury—the doctors recommend it.

1416 Beverly Road
Brooklyn, NY 111226
718-469-3377
www.ELNOEL.com

Carapan

Carapan, a unique healing and massage center just north of Greenwich Village, has captured so much of the mystical essence of the native Southwest, you'll feel as if you've stepped into a shaman's sacred pueblo in Taos. The air is strong with the scent of burning mesquite, pinon and juniper incense. The raw wood lockers, wide plank flooring and rustic walls are cut from fragrant cedar. Native American flute music and chants play subtly in the background, while sepia photos of the great chiefs watch nearby.

Being transported to the calming deserts outside Sante Fe for an hour or two is just the thing for keeping your spirit alive in New York.

5 West 16th Street
Bet. 5th and 6th Avenues
Phone: 212-633-6220

Soho Sanctuary

White washed walls, soft pine floors, enormous windows resplendent with foliage, and the subtle scents of jasmine and lavender lend the landmark Soho Loft an air of nature's serenity.

A women-only day spa, Soho Sanctuary combines mindful movement practices such as yoga and the Alexander Technique with spa treatments including Dr. Haushka facials, shiatsu massage in the circular meditation room, hot stone massage, one-on-one thai yoga massage, aromatherapy massage, and reflexology. Beauty and renewal don't require elaborate machines or regimes, but rather a commitment to love and care for yourself and those around you. This spa goes deeper than pampering your skin; it nourishes a healthy sense of self.

119 Mercer Street, 3rd Floor
bet. Prince and Spring Streets
Phone: 212-334-5550

about the Authors

✣ Beth Donnelly Cabán
   teaches yoga and meditation.
   She lives in Brooklyn.

✣ Andrea Martin
   lives in New York City
   where she teaches high school,
   practices yoga, meditates,
   and makes art.

✣ Allan Ishac
   is the author of
   New York's 50 Best
   Places to Find
   Peace and Quiet
   and *New York's 50 Best*
   Places to Take Children.

NEW YORK'S 50 BEST SERIES

GUIDES
TO THE
BEST OF
NEW YORK

New York's New & Avant-Garde Art Galleries $14.00

New York's 50 Best Art in Public Places $12.00

New York's 50 Best Places to Go Birding $15.00

New York's 50 Best Bookstores for Book Lovers $12.00

New York's 50 Best Places to Discover and Enjoy in Central Park $12.00

New York's 50 Best Places to Take Children $12.00

New York's 60 Best Wonderful Little Hotels $15.00

New York's 50 Best Places to Have a Kid's Party $12.00

New York's 50 Best Museums for Cool Parents and Their Kids $14.00

New York's 75 Best Nights Out:
Fabulous and Funky to Just Plain Fun $12.00

New York's 100 Best Party Places $14.00

New York's 50 Best Places to Find Peace & Quiet $12.00

New York's 100 Best Little Places to Shop $15.00

New York's 50 Best Skyscrapers $12.00

Brooklyn's Best: Happy Wandering in the Borough of Kings $14.00

You can find these and other City & Company titles at your local bookstore,
through booksellers on the web, or by contacting City & Company.

City & Company   22 West 23rd Street   New York, NY 10010
Tel: 212.366.1988   Fax: 212.242.0415
Email: cityco@mindspring.com   www.cityandcompany.com